MW00422855

JEFFREY'S FAVORITE
13 GHOST STORIES

ALSO BY KATHRYN TUCKER WINDHAM

Treasured Alabama Recipes (1967)
13 Alabama Ghosts and Jeffrey (1969)
Jeffrey Introduces 13 More Southern Ghosts (1971)
Treasured Tennessee Recipes (1972)
Treasured Georgia Recipes (1973)
13 Georgia Ghosts and Jeffrey (1973)
13 Mississippi Ghosts and Jeffrey (1974)
Exploring Alabama (1974)
Alabama: One Big Front Porch (1975)
13 Tennessee Ghosts and Jeffrey (1977)
The Ghost in the Sloss Furnaces (1978)
Southern Cooking to Remember (1978)
Count Those Buzzards! Stamp Those Grey Mules! (1979)
Jeffrey's Latest 13: More Alabama Ghosts (1982)
A Serigamy of Stories (1983)
Odd–Egg Editor (1990)
The Autobiography of a Bell (1991)
A Sampling of Selma Stories (1991)
My Name is Julia (1991)
Twice Blessed (1996)
Encounters (1998)
The Bridal Wreath Bush (1999)
Common Threads (2000)
It's Christmas! (2002)
Ernest's Gift (2004)

Jeffrey's Favorite 13 Ghost Stories

KATHRYN TUCKER WINDHAM

NewSouth Books
Montgomery

NewSouth Books
P.O. Box 1588
Montgomery, AL 36102

Library of Congress Cataloging-in-Publication Data

Windham, Kathryn Tucker.
Jeffrey's favorite 13 ghost stories / Kathryn Tucker Windham.
p. cm.
ISBN 1-58838-170-6 (alk. paper)
1. Ghosts—Southern States. 2. Haunted places—Southern States.
I. Title: Jeffrey's favorite thirteen ghost stories. II. Title.
BF1472.U6W563 2004
133.1'0975—dc22
2004021194

Design by Randall Williams

Printed in the United States of America
by the Maple-Vail Book Manufacturing Group

IN MEMORY

OF

MY FRIEND HERMAN MOORE
1927–2003

BOOKSELLER AND LIBRARY EVANGELIST

AND

JEFFREY'S BEST FRIEND

CONTENTS

Preface

*I*t has been nearly forty years since Jeffrey came clumping into my life. Then, back in 1966, I did not know who or what was walking with heavy steps down the hall, opening and slamming doors, moving a variety of objects, rocking in a rocking chair, and frightening our old cat, Hornblower. Hornblower, now deceased, was the only living thing ever frightened by Jeffrey.

One of my children gave the intruder his name. The name was chosen for no particular reason, but we were pleased years later to learn that one of England's most famous ghosts was named Jeffrey. The English Jeffrey haunted the rectory in Epworth where John and Charles Wesley, the founders of Methodism, lived.

Our family has a real affection for Jeffrey. We're comfortable, even grateful, having him around. We blame everything that goes wrong on Jeffrey, thus relieving ourselves of any responsibility for such mishaps as spilled food, forgotten appointments, lost car keys, smudged handwriting, and such.

Soon after Jeffrey attached himself to our family, I went over to Montgomery to talk to Margaret Gillis Figh, longtime folklore teacher at Huntingdon College, about his presence in our home.

Our conversation naturally conjured up other tales of Alabama ghosts. Before our visit ended, we, possibly with a bit of prodding by Jeffrey, were talking seriously about selecting thirteen of our state's best ghost tales and writing a book about them. We proposed to call our book "13 Alabama Ghosts and Jeffrey."

We dared not offend Jeffrey by failing to include his name in the title!

My friends Helen and David Strode Akens, who owned The Strode Publishers in Huntsville, published our book in 1969. Much to our surprise, the book we thought we had written for adult readers became very popular with elementary school pupils. It still is.

Jeffrey provided a second surprise when, after the publication of *13 Alabama Ghosts and Jeffrey,* I became almost obsessed by a sense of urgency to collect and preserve true ghost stories from throughout the South. For a quarter of a century, not full time, of course, I traveled around the South seeking out the tellers of such stories and investigating half-forgotten mysteries.

Whenever I let other projects interfere with ghost-gathering, Jeffrey would become very active, as though he were reprimanding me for failing to attend to my mission.

As a result of Jeffrey's nagging persuasion, I wrote five more collections of Southern ghost stories: *13 Mississippi Ghosts and Jeffrey, 13 Tennessee Ghosts and Jeffrey, 13 Georgia Ghosts and Jeffrey, Jeffrey Introduces 13 More Southern Ghosts* and *Jeffrey's Latest 13: More Alabama Ghosts,* all published by Strode. They sold well until a fire destroyed the publishing company.

The six collections had been out of print for more than two years when the University of Alabama Press began publishing and distributing them again. The arrangement worked well until financial restraints made it unprofitable for the University Press to continue publishing the series. With the exception of *13 Alabama Ghosts and Jeffrey*, the ghost books went out of print.

This turn of events upset Jeffrey. He became very assertive, seemingingly demanding that I arrange to keep some of his favorite stories in print. So I have. With the help of my family, readers of various ages and the editors at NewSouth, thirteen stories were selected from the five out-of-print books to be included in this new volume.

Jeffrey hopes readers approve of the selections. So do I.

K.T.W.

Jeffrey's Favorite 13 Ghost Stories

Jeffrey's Favorite 13 Ghost Stories

1

I'll Never Leave You

<small>FAYETTE COUNTY, ALABAMA</small>

*M*any communities in Alabama have local legends about strange images that have appeared on tombstones, mysterious markings with no logical explanations.

There is, for example, the story from Red Level about a man who, many years ago, was riding horseback when his horse ran away, and the man's head got caught in the forks of a low-hanging tree limb. He was killed instantly. The image of a man hanging from a tree limb appeared on the rider's tombstone soon after his grave was put in place, the story goes.

Other areas have their own images of devils' heads and black cats and grinning skulls and such that have formed on tombstones. Each of these supposedly supernatural pictures has its own story, a story told and retold, changing gradually with the retellings.

Some of these silhouettes are associated with romantic events, tragic love stories of long ago. One of the best known of this type is the figure of the young girl that appeared on the tombstone of Robert Musgrove over in Fayette County many years ago.

The Musgroves were among the pioneer settlers in northwest Alabama, moving there from the Carolinas with the final wave of emigrants in the 1820s. They brought their household goods and their farming equipment in wagons, jouncing along over the rough roads hewn through the wilderness. They came to stay.

Some members of the family stopped in Walker County while others continued their journey into northern Fayette County where they settled along Luxapallila Creek.

Just as there were differences in opinion among the family as to where to settle, there were sharper differences in loyalties when the War Between the States came along. Many Musgroves served proudly in the Confederate forces while many others remained staunch Unionists. It was a bitter and bloody time with deaths from ambush, torture, hangings, house burnings, and beatings reported frequently (and many not reported at all) in those isolated, wooded hills.

The scars of that conflict had not yet begun to heal when Robert L. Musgrove was born in September 1866. As a boy, he heard stories of death and plunder when armed guerrilla bands enforced their own brands of justice, and he listened to the names of his own kinsman cast as heroes and villains in those outrages.

As did the other youngsters in his neighborhood, Robert helped his parents with the work on their farm, found time to roam in the woods and along the creek, and attended church at Musgrove Chapel every preaching Sunday.

Members of Robert's family were dedicated Methodists, and, very soon after their arrival in Fayette County, they built a log church which they named Musgrove Chapel. The benches were uncomfortable, and the one-room building was hot in the summer and cold in the wintertime, but the Musgroves filled those rough benches to hear The Word proclaimed, and if their bodies suffered, their souls were revived.

Or so they told Robert.

Robert, looking down the benches at the Sabbath gatherings of Musgroves, wondered if his kin had in truth been involved in the atrocities he heard about. He tried to imagine what the men looked like when they were younger.

Musgrove men, old timers recall, were invariably handsome. They, most of them, were tall and muscular, and they moved with the ease and grace peculiar to the outdoorsmen they were. They had ruddy complexions, dark hair, and bluish-grey eyes. It was a pleasing combination.

As he grew older, Robert Musgrove became the handsomest of all the clan. On those rare occasions when he went to town—to Winfield or to Fayette Courthouse or even as far away as Tuscaloosa—it is reported that every woman who saw him walking along the streets stared after him as long as he was in sight and then sighed, "Aaaaahh," softly and longingly.

Robert, they say, never even noticed those stares or heard those sighs. Though he, his friends said, could have had his choice of any beauty in northwest

Alabama or northeast Mississippi, Robert wasn't interested in girls at all then, not seriously. His mind was on trains.

Ever since he saw his first train (there is a difference of opinion over whether this event occurred in Tuscaloosa or in Columbus, Mississippi), Robert Musgrove was obsessed with interest in steam locomotives.

He purely fell in love with trains. "I'm going to be a train engineer," he announced. Trains were all he ever thought about. An engineer was all he ever wanted to be.

As soon as he was old enough (maybe earlier since birth certificates and child labor laws and such had not been heard of then), Robert got a job on the railroad. He started as water boy for a crew laying tracks, some folks recall, but Robert didn't object to the hard, menial labor. The only thing that mattered to him was that he was working on the railroad.

He was as proud as a man could be when the Georgia Pacific Railway Company opened a line to Fayette in 1883, the first railroad in his home county. Until that time, Tuscaloosa and Columbus, Mississippi, had been the nearest rail terminals to the county seat.

"Now some of my kinfolks can find out how important railroads are," Robert commented. To him, railroads were still the center of his universe.

Robert returned to his family home every now and then, when he had time off from work. If his visits were on Sunday, he always joined his kinfolks and friends for worship services at Musgrove Chapel. After church, when worshippers gathered in cluster to talk a bit before heading home, Robert took pride in telling them about his railroad career.

The St. Louis and San Francisco Railroad was Robert's road, the one he worked for. He had a good boarding place in Memphis, Tennessee, and he was assigned to the run between Memphis and Amory, Mississippi. Robert worked as conductor, brakeman, fireman, and after a good many years passed, he achieved his lifelong ambition: he became a railroad engineer.

Robert, associates say, treated his engines as though they were living, loving things, as though the engines understood his respect and affection for them. And the engines responded to Robert Musgrove's attentions.

"His engines could do almost anything. They seemed almost to anticipate his expectations, as though they were trained animals instead of masses of metal," they said.

After Robert became an engineer, he relaxed a bit and began diversifying his interests. He discovered, among other things, that girls are nice. And he wished he had made that pleasant discovery earlier: Robert was already well into his thirties then.

For a while, Robert had many girlfriends. He was still quite handsome, as all Musgrove men are handsome, and his career as an engineer made him even more attractive to women. So Robert enjoyed his popularity. He had a good time with his female admirers in Memphis, and he delighted in his feminine friends in Amory. There were also a good many young ladies between those two cities whose company Robert Musgrove treasured.

He wasn't quite sure when or how it happened, but a beautiful young woman in Amory captured his heart. It wasn't long before he was thinking of marriage and a home and a family—brand new thoughts for him. Robert had lost none of his enthusiasm for railroading, but love had opened new vistas of joy.

Miracle of miracles, the woman he loved also loved him. When he asked her to become his wife, she accepted. It was spring, the loveliest spring Robert Musgrove had ever known.

He acted like a love-smitten youngster, associates recall, even when he was at work. "Listen to my whistle," he said to his fireman. "Listen. Know what it's saying? It says, 'I'm in love. I'm in love.' I'm going to blow it all the way from Memphis to Amory!" He wanted the whole listening world to know about his happiness.

Then, one dreary night in April 1904, Robert Musgrove was killed in a head-on collision with another train between Memphis and Amory.

A man on horseback brought the sad news to his family in northern Fayette County.

Arrangements were made to hold Robert Musgrove's funeral services at Musgrove Chapel, the church where he had worshipped in childhood. His body was sent by train from Memphis to Winfield, the nearest rail point to Musgrove Chapel. This was before the days of automobiles, so a caravan of wagons met the funeral train at Winfield to transport Robert's body and the contingent of his friends who accompanied it out to Musgrove Chapel.

Robert's boyhood friends drove some of those wagons. As they waited at the Winfield station for the train to arrive, they talked about Robert, their memories of their good times together.

"Hard to believe Robert is dead," they said again and again "But if he had to die, it's good to know he died at the throttle of his train. He would have wanted it that way."

When the train pulled into the station, the friends walked quietly to the baggage car, lifted Robert's coffin out, and placed it in the lead wagon. Then they spoke to Robert's railroad friends who had come to his funeral and made sure that these visitors were comfortably seated in the wagon for the ride in the country. Among the mourners who came on that train was the young woman to whom Robert had been engaged. She rode to the church in the wagon driven by W. L. Moss.

"She was a beautiful young woman. So sad," he recalled years later. "I'll never forget how she looked all dressed in black."

Other people who met her remember thinking how tragic that she should be forced to wear the doleful black of mourning instead of the joyous white of a wedding dress.

The small chapel was filled to overflowing that afternoon with people who cared about Robert Musgrove and who grieved over his death. The alter area of the chapel was crowded with flowers, formal floral arrangements from the city mixed with fresh blossoms (jonquils, pear blossoms, yellow forsythias, and such) cut from Fayette County yards.

The preacher used the Methodist ritual for the burial of the dead, and he read the Twenty-Third Psalm and John 14:1, "Let not your heart be troubled . . ." and he talked about how life is like a railroad. The choir sang "In the Sweet By and By" and "When They Ring the Golden Bells."

Then all the people went out into the graveyard with the preacher leading the way and the pallbearers walking slowly and solemnly behind him.

After the pallbearers had lowered the coffin into the grave and the preacher had said the final words and the grave had been filled, most of the people left the graveyard and started home. They grieved about Robert, but there were chores to do. The scattering of folks who loitered after the burial saw Robert's sweetheart kneel beside the fresh grave. She folded her hands and bowed her head, and she remained motionless in that attitude of prayer for several minutes. As she arose, people close by heard her whisper, "Robert, I'll never leave you."

Nobody now remembers her name, but nobody who witnessed the sad drama ever forgot how she knelt at the grave or her whispered promise of eternal love.

Several months after Robert's death, his family had an impressive granite marker erected at his grave, an eight-foot obelisk. Robert would have liked it.

In the years that followed, worshippers at Musgrove chapel and families who lived nearby noticed that periodically Robert Musgrove's grave was cleared of weeds and fallen twigs, and fresh flowers were on his grave.

The flowers were floral arrangements, not bouquets from local gardens.

"Robert's sweetheart must have been here," the observers commented. And they told again of the events surrounding Robert's funeral, of how his sweetheart whispered, "Robert, I'll never leave you."

Years passed, and the periodic evidences of care for Robert Musgrove's grave continued. Then, as time went by, some woman in the community noticed that there had been no fresh flowers on Robert's grave in a long time. She commented to a friend on the long absence of flowers.

"Well," the friend replied, "just think how many years it has been since Robert died. His sweetheart must be dead now, too. If she's not dead, she must be too old and feeble to visit the grave. She kept her promise for many years though, didn't she?" Then one Sunday in 1962 as worshippers were coming out of Musgrove Chapel at the close of the morning service, someone glanced over into the graveyard.

"What's that on Robert Musgrove's tombstone?" she asked. "It looks like a shadow of some kind."

Several people, prodded by curiosity, walked into

the cemetery to get a closer look. There on Robert Musgrove's tombstone they saw the distinct silhouette of a young girl. Her head was bowed and her hands were folded as if in prayer. The silhouette was so distinct that the viewers could see her hair piled high on her head. Even the curve of her eyelashes was quite plain.

"It's Robert Musgrove's sweetheart!" an older man in the group exclaimed. "That's just the way she looked when she knelt on Robert's grave and promised, 'Robert, I'll never leave you.' I was just a boy, but I saw her and heard her—and I'll never forget it."

News of the image of the young girl on Robert Musgrove's grave marker spread quickly throughout that part of Alabama, and curiosity seekers by the hundreds swarmed to the country churchyard.

The invasion of strangers upset members of the Musgrove family, and they tried to remove the image from the stone. But though they scoured and rubbed and scrubbed, the image would not come off. Finally they sent to Birmingham for a stonemason to sandblast the figure from the granite.

With the image gone, the unwelcome visitors

stopped coming to the cemetery, and talk in the community turned to other things.

But the image returned, as plain as ever. Again the story of the lover's promise was told, and again the throngs of strangers came to look and wonder.

The stonemason returned to clean the stone. When he left, the tall marker was as white and unsullied as the day it was put in place.

With the figure gone from tombstone, the crowds again lost interest in the grave and in its link to the supernatural.

But, they say, the likeness of the grieving sweetheart slowly returned on the surface of the tombstone until, once again, it was as well defined as it had been the day it first appeared.

"She loved Robert very much," the tellers of the story say. "Her love was as strong as her promise, 'Robert, I'll never leave you.'"

2

The Locket

RENFROE (TALLADEGA COUNTY), ALABAMA

*N*one of his descendants now knows why Jacob Hammer left his native Indiana and moved to Alabama. They do know from records in family Bibles that Jacob Hammer was living in Talladega County when he married Martha Louisa Hicks of Renfroe on December 1, 1887. He was thirty-four at the time of their marriage, and his bride was twenty-one.

Mr. Hammer had taught school and had been engaged in merchandising in Indiana, and family tradition says he taught school, ran a store, and farmed after he came to Alabama.

In the first six years of their marriage, five children were born to the couple: Cassandra, William Benjamin, Emma Everett, Diana, and Dixie Homer. Some of the children's names, family members point out, reflect Mr. Hammer's interest in Greek and Roman mythology. He was interested in many things. He wanted to call his first child by her full name, Cassandra, but his wife, who cared little for the classics, insisted on calling her Cassie, and Cassie she became.

Cassie was nine years old when her baby brother, Harvey, was born. She was a "big girl" then, old enough and responsible enough to take over much of the care of the new baby. Being the oldest in the family—and being a girl—Cassie at nine knew how to cook, clean house, wash clothes, iron, milk the cow, kill and dress a chicken, sew, mend and darn, and take care of the younger children.

They were living in the community of Stemley, near the Coosa River, in Talladega County then. All the children from Cassie to Harvey were born there, but the town has now dwindled into nothingness, and only a few older people remember where it was.

Cassie Hammer was likely too busy helping her mother care for the younger children, especially the baby, to have much time to play, but she really didn't mind. There was something different about taking care of Harvey, something that soothed her resentment over having the responsibilities of a grown-up forced so early upon her.

Harvey was a good baby. And he was beautiful.

"Look, Mama," Cassie would say after she had bathed and dressed him. "Look how beautiful Harvey is! I wish I had curly hair like he has. Look how it shines in the sunlight. And look how big his eyes are. Sometimes I think he sees things we can't see. What do you suppose he sees, Mama?"

Mrs. Hammer, being a sensible woman, replied, "Don't be silly, Cassie. He sees just what we see. Nothing else." She paused. "But he is a beautiful baby. I wish I could have his picture made, looking just the way he looks now: all clean and shining and happy."

She took the baby in her arms and kissed him. It was not easy for Mrs. Hammer to show affection, it wasn't her nature, but Harvey had a quality, an elusive quality that even his mother couldn't define, that called her to hug him and to cuddle him and to call him "my precious baby."

Everybody loved Harvey. They loved him not merely because he was the youngest in the family, but because Harvey himself was so loving. His arms went out to everyone who came near, his smile had a radiance of pure joy, and his laughter was as musical and refreshing as snatches of dancing tunes.

Even Jacob Hammer, usually too busy earning a living for his growing family to squander time in play, would bounce his baby on his knee and sing to him some half-forgotten songs from his Indiana boyhood, and talk to him about matters only the two of them understood.

"You know what?" Jacob asked his wife. "This son of ours will grow up to see flying machines carrying passengers and mail from city to city. And he'll ride on wide thoroughfares connecting the cities. Big changes are coming in this world—and Harvey will be part of them."

"Oh, Jacob!" Mrs. Hammer replied. "What a wild imagination you have! How do you ever think of such foolish things?"

"They're not foolish," Jacob stated firmly. "They'll come true. You'll see—if you live long enough. Harvey believes what I'm telling you. Don't you, Harvey?"

The baby smiled, and his eyes shone as though he did indeed understand, as though he shared with his father an exciting look into the future.

Harvey was walking and beginning to talk a little when the family moved to Renfroe, a community some six miles west of Talladega. At that time, Mr. Hammer was devoting most of his energies to farming.

Cassie continued to be Harvey's loving protector, and the toddler adored her. Mrs. Hammer may have been a little jealous, but she tried not to show it.

"I hope your own babies will love you as much as Harvey does," she said to Cassie one day.

"He loves you, too, Mama," Cassie replied. "He loves everybody—but you most of all. Sometimes," she added, "I think it's not me but my gold locket that Harvey loves. He plays with it every time I wear it, and I believe he wants to wear it himself!"

Cassie's locket, her only piece of jewelry had been a gift from her father. It was heart shaped and hung on a slender gold chain.

"It looks like you," Jacob Hammer had said as he

fastened it around her neck. "It looks like my Cassandra."

Even then Harvey reached out to get the shining locket.

"No, Harvey," Cassie said gently. "Boys don't wear lockets. This is mine. Maybe some time I'll let you try it on. But not now!"

One stormy night in late September 1898 Cassie woke up and heard Harvey crying in her parents' bedroom. She ran across the hall and found her mother holding Harvey in her lap while Mr. Hammer rubbed the little boy's chest with melted tallow and wrapped a flannel cloth around him.

"It's the croup," Mrs. Hammer told Cassie. "He's real sick." She held the baby close and rocked him.

Harvey was limp and listless, and his breathing was raspy.

"What can I do?" Cassie asked.

"Nothing," Mrs. Hammer replied. "We've done all we can. Now we will just have to wait."

Just as daylight marked the end of that long night, Harvey Hammer died. He was twenty months old.

When word of the child's death spread through

the community, the neighbors came, as they always came in the rural South. They were silent with grief, some of them, while others tried to speak comfortingly about "understanding some day" and "God's will." Jacob Hammer did not believe it was God's will for Harvey to die. Neither did Cassie.

The younger children walked around the house big-eyed and frightened until an aunt came to take them home with her.

Mrs. Hammer's grief was too deep for tears. "My baby. My precious baby," she kept repeating. "He's dead. And we don't even have a picture of him. We never had a picture made of our precious Harvey."

Mr. Hammer, hoping to ease his wife's sorrow, promised, "We'll send in to Talladega and get the photographer to come out and take Harvey's picture in his coffin. Then you—all of us—will have his picture to remember him by."

Outside, a cold, slashing rain seemed almost an extension of the gloominess of the household.

Men who lived nearby fashioned a small coffin from pine boards, and the women padded it with cotton and lined it with soft white cloth.

Those same neighbor women made a little dress for Harvey to be buried in. It was white, as befitted a burial garment for a pure child, and it had a wide, ruffled, lace-trimmed collar. When they put the garment on him, the neck was too big, making the collar hang low on his pale shoulders.

"That will be all right," one of the women said. "When we put him in the coffin, we'll just pull the collar in place and tuck the extra fullness under him."

And they did. After Havey's body was placed in the coffin, and after the seamstresses had pulled up the collar and tucked it beneath him, nobody could tell the neck was too large.

"He looks so peaceful," the people said. "Just like he was asleep. Come look at your little brother, Cassie," they said.

Cassie looked. She knew the women were expecting her to say something, but she couldn't make any words come. She stood there silent for a long time, just looking at Harvey and wondering what it was like to be dead. Then, very slowly, she took off her heart-shaped locket and fastend it around Harvey's neck.

The rain never slacked.

Finally word came that the roads between Talladega and Renfroe were impassable, so the photographer couldn't come. Harvey Hammer was buried without ever having had his picture made.

His mother continued to grieve, as did other members of the family, and she continued to weep over having no picture of her little boy.

"If only I had his picture to look at, to remember him by," she moaned.

A few weeks after Harvey's death, Mr. Hammer set out to clear a parcel of land some distance from his house. The land was too far away for him to go and come from home each day, so he made arrangements to camp in an abandoned one-room schoolhouse near the property. The building had a pot-bellied stove in it that he could use for heat and for cooking, so Mr. Hammer took a cot to sleep on, blankets, some food, and moved into the school.

The first night there, he was tired from the move and from the strenuous labor of clearing the land, and he fell asleep soon after he had eaten supper. He had been asleep for some time when he was awakened by a brilliant light.

His first thought was that the building was on fire, and he jumped up to run outside.

But as soon as he was fully awake, he realized that the building was not on fire. The light came from a corner of the room. In the corner was his little boy, Harvey, holding a burning candle.

Jacob Hammer walked toward the figure and reached out toward him. As he did, the child blew out the candle and vanished.

There was no more sleep for Jacob Hammer that night. Questions crowded in upon him: had he really seen his son or was his grief conjuring up cruel visions? Could Harvey have returned from the dead? And if so, why?

The daylight brought no answers and the questions haunted him all the next day as he worked in his field.

That second night, the same thing happened: he was awakened by a flash of light and saw Harvey, holding a flickering candle, in the corner of the room. Once again Jacob Hammer approached the child, and once again the child blew out the candle and vanished.

As Jacob Hammer lay awake and tried to answer the questions that trampled through his mind, a new thought came to him. Was it possible, he wondered, that Harvey's spirit was so disturbed by his mother's yearning for a picture of him that he had come back so that such a picture could be made? The more he thought about it, the more he became convinced of the logic of his theory.

So when daylight came, instead of going to his field, Jacob Hammer went into Talladega to borrow a camera from W.H. McMillan, a photographer there.

He did not tell Mr. McMillan why he wanted to use the camera. He would have felt foolish saying that he intended to try to photograph a ghost, so he implied that he needed a picture of a landmark on his property, and he promised to return the camera early the next morning.

Mr. McMillan let him borrow one of the cumbersome old cameras with a tripod, and he showed him how to use it.

"Be careful with the glass negative," he warned. "They break right easy."

Jacob Hammer took the equipment back to the

school building and set it up beside his cot, focusing it on the corner where he had seen the apparition on the two previous nights. He did not go to sleep that night: he sat on the side of the cot and waited.

Hours passed. Nothing happened. Mr. Hammer was beginning to wonder if he had imagined the whole thing when suddenly a bright light filled the room, and he saw Harvey in the far corner. He snapped the shutter of the camera, and the figure disappeared.

Mr. Hammer dozed fitfully (he was very tired) until daylight came. Then he went to Talladega to return the camera and to have the glass plate developed. Once again he wondered what he should tell the photographer, and once again he decided to tell him nothing.

After he had thanked the man for the use of the camera, he asked, "Will you please develop the plate? I took only one picture, but I would very much like to see it."

Jacob Hammer waited, a restless wait, until Mr. McMillan came out of the darkroom. He was holding the glass negative, still wet, up to the light.

"Jacob," he said, "I thought you did not have a

picture of your little boy, the one who died."

"We don't have," Jacob Hammer replied.

"Yes, you do. This is him—Harvey—right here. Look."

Jacob Hammer looked. On the negative was the exact likeness of Harvey Hammer: blond curls, big eyes, wistful smile framed in a strange aura of light.

Jacob Hammer was unable to speak. He took the negative from the hands of the puzzled photographer and hastened home.

"Martha! Martha!" he shouted as he ran into the house. "Look!" He held the glass negative up to the light.

Martha Hammer looked and burst into sobs. "It's Harvey! It's my baby's picture!"

Cassie and the other children came running to see what was happening.

"It's Harvey!" they said. "Harvey. Just like he looked."

"And look," Cassie said, "look how his dress has fallen around his shoulders. And look around his neck—that's my heart-shaped locket, the one I put on him!"

After the family had seen the negative with the likeness of Harvey on it and after he had told the story of how he had made the picture, Jacob Hammer took the glass plate back to the photographer in Talladega to have prints made from it.

Three of those prints made in the fall of 1898 still exist. Each one, though faded by time, shows quite distinctly the head and shoulders of a beautiful blond child with wandering eyes that seem to peer into another world. The lace-trimmed collar of his white garment has slipped down around his shoulders. And round his neck hangs a gold, heart-shaped locket.

3

A Promise Kept

SUGGSVILLE, ALABAMA

*N*obody in Suggsville was surprised when Stephen Cleveland took off for California to look for gold. Fact is, most of his friends would have been disappointed if Stephen had not been a part of the 1849 gold rush.

"Just like him," they said. "Let Stephen hear about any excitement going on, and he wants to be a part of it—even if he has to go all the way to California!"

Stephen didn't get in on the first of the California gold fever because news of the discovery of the precious metal at Sutter's Mill was a long time reaching the Clarke County town of Suggsville. It was several months after the discovery that Stephen Cleveland heard stories of the rich gold fields around San Francisco and of the men who were making fortunes there.

As soon as he heard those stories, Stephen was impatient to join the other prospectors heading west. He did not have to ask permission of anybody (he was twenty-two years old, a man grown), so he packed what clothes he figured he would need, tucked what money he had into a wide belt around his waist, and went to tell his family good-bye before he set out to seek his fortunes in California.

His father, James Cleveland, gave Stephen a few parting words of fatherly advice. He knew Stephen was not really listening, but he felt morally obligated to pass along some bits of wisdom to his son. James Cleveland was a staunch Baptist.

So, with his father's advice and with the envious good wishes of his friends, Stephen Cleveland headed west to become a part of a horde of adventurers, many of them young men about his own age, willing to gamble all they owned on the chance of striking it rich in the gold country.

As James Cleveland watched his son ride away, he recalled earlier occasions when he had given unheeded advice to Stephen. For though Stephen had not been an obstreperous child, he was adventurous, headstrong, and reckless. It was Stephen who, though duly warned of the dangers by his father, climbed the tallest trees, rode the wildest horses, and swam the swiftest streams. He had an assortment of scars to show for his exploits, but he had no regrets. "You know I had to try it, Papa," he would say when his father reproved him. "I was scared, so I had to do it. You wouldn't want me to be a coward, would you?"

There was a time when Stephen, about ten years old, planned a reenactment of the Canoe Fight. He, of course, would take the role of Sam Dale, hero of the miniature naval battle. He cast his playmates in the roles of the other participants, though it took a fight or two to persuade some of the boys to play Indians, and he located canoes to use in the drama. The long overland march to the Alabama River was about to begin when James Cleveland learned of Stephen's plans and ordered the group to disband.

"The river is too dangerous to play in," he told them.

Stephen obeyed his father that day. But the following day, while his father was supervising some work on the far side of the plantation, he assembled his cast again and lead them to a creek. "Papa didn't say anything about playing in the creek," he assured them as he directed the mock battle between the boatload of Indian warriors and the heroes in the canoe.

There were some casualties in the make-believe war, nothing serious, but enough bruises, scrapes, sore heads, and wet and torn clothes to prompt parents to ask questions.

James Cleveland was furious when news of Stephen's escapade reached him. But he forgave him, as he always did, and, later, he even laughed about the episode.

Joining the California gold rush was adventure tailor-made for Stephen.

Weeks and weeks passed with no word from Stephen, but nobody worried about him. He could take care of himself. Always had.

When Stephen got home from California, he looked taller and more muscular than when he had left, and he had a new air of confidence, the look of a man who had run into rough times and had dealt with

them courageously. He wasn't cocky, just self-assured.

He didn't bring back saddlebags full of gold nuggets, but he did bring back a score of stories about the places he had been and the people he had met and the experiences he had had.

Stephen also brought back plans for a house.

"I saw a house I liked out there, and I had an architect draw me some plans for one like it," Stephen said. "It's a different kind of house, a good house, and I want one like it. You'll see what it's like when I get it built." He made it plain that he did not want to show his plans or to talk further about his house. When friends asked questions, he replied, "Just wait until I get it built."

It was a rather long wait.

Stephen Cleveland did not build his house until 1860. There were a good many other things he had to do first.

He had entered the practice of law, opening his office in Suggsville, and he had also become involved in politics. He campaigned first for some of his friends when they ran for office, and later he himself ran for the Alabama Senate and was elected to represent the Second Senatorial District (Clarke, Monroe, and Baldwin Counties). He resigned from the senate in 1861 to enter military service.

There were family obligations, too. Stephen Cleveland married Eliza Creagh, daughter of his neighbor Gerard Wathall Creagh. On August 6, 1856, their first child, a son named Walter, was born.

That son, friends said, completely changed Stephen's life.

"Stephen acts as if he's the only papa in the world!" his friends laughed. "To hear him talk, you'd think nobody else ever had a son. Nothing else is as important to him as that baby is."

Stephen was, indeed a doting father. As soon as Walter could sit up, he took the baby on his horse with him and rode at a canter down the main street of Suggsville. He stopped frequently to introduce his son to friends along the way, to show the baby off. When they returned home, he handed the baby to a nurse and said to Eliza:

"You would have been proud of him—he never cried once! Rode as if he had been born in the saddle.

He'll have to have his own pony before long."

Eliza smiled at her husband as she took the baby from the nurse's arms. "Don't hurry with that pony, please. He is a baby yet!"

Walter was still little more than a baby when his sister, Lillian, was born. As soon as he laid eyes on her, Stephen set out to inform everybody he met that Lillian was the most beautiful daughter a man ever had. He believed it, too.

But though he loved her devotedly and catered to her every wish, it was Walter who rode on his horse with him, galloping along the Old Line Road or trotting between the long cotton rows on the plantation; it was Walter who went fishing with him and who "helped" skin the deer he shot; it was Walter who listened to his stories and who learned all the verses of some rather risqué songs.

Sometimes Stephen expected too much of his little son. The summer he was almost four, Stephen took Walter to the creek to teach him to swim. The dark brown water frightened the child, and he cried.

"I'm scared, Papa," he sobbed.

"That's all right, Walter," Stephen soothed him.

"Don't ever be ashamed of being afraid. You may be afraid, but you are not a coward. There's a difference. Come here and let me hold you in the water."

Before the afternoon was over, Walter was dog-paddling in the creek, no longer afraid. And very proud.

It was that same summer, the summer of 1860, that Eliza and Stephen's house was being completed. Stephen had brought out his plans, had purchased the required material, and he spent much of the summer supervising the skilled artisans who did the work. The site he chose for the house was on land his wife inherited at her father's death.

The house was, indeed, unusual. It was a one-story, L-shaped building only one room deep. Each of the rooms opened onto the front porch and the back porch, giving each room the cross-ventilation so welcome during Southern summers.

The porches were wide with cypress balusters, and the front porch had two sets of steps, one on the north side and one on the east. Those porches were perfect places for children to play.

Once when Stephen had Walter on the horse with

him, he urged the horse up the front steps on the east, around the porch, and down the north steps. Walter was delighted: "Do it again! Do it again, please, Papa!" he begged. But Eliza was not pleased. She ran out on the porch and shook her long skirts at them.

"Keep your horse where it belongs!" she shouted at Stephen. She knew he had already ridden out of earshot, but she felt better for having shown her displeasure. Stephen, though he could not hear his wife, knew what she was saying, and he laughed at her display of anger.

Stephen Cleveland was a happy man. He had a fine family, his law practice was flourishing, his agricultural interests were profitable, he had built the house he wanted, and he was a successful politician. Life was good.

Then came The War.

In January 1861, Governor Andrew Moore seized the federal forts and arsenals in the state, including Fort Morgan and Fort Gaines. On January 11, 1861, Stephen Cleveland joined his fellow legislators in Montgomery in passing the Ordinance of Secession.

Walter met him on the porch when he returned

home from that legislative session. "I missed you, Papa," he said. "Please don't go away again." Stephen lifted his son and gave him a swift hug.

"You're about to get too big for me to pick you up, Walter! You're growing up too fast. I missed you, too." His face became grave. "I wish I could stay here with you and Lillian and Mama, wish I could stay forever, but I have to go away again. The South needs me, and I'll have to go fight. But not right now," he added quickly, seeing the tears about to fill his son's eyes.

"Won't you be scared?" Walter asked.

"Yes, I'll be scared. But I'm not a coward, so I'll go and do my duty for the South."

The next weeks were busy times for Stephen Cleveland. Many business matters had to be settled, legislative affairs required his attention, and arrangements had to be made for the protection of his family before he could volunteer for the new Confederate Army.

It was April, military records show, when Stephen left Suggsville for Fort Morgan on Mobile Bay. He served as captain of a company of Clarke County infantry with the Second Alabama regiment.

On the day he left for Fort Morgan, the children, worn out from a morning of play, were taking a nap. Eliza started into their room to wake them so that they could tell their father good-bye, but Stephen stopped her.

"No," he said, "don't get them up. Let them sleep. I am a coward, I suppose—I can't bear to say good-bye to them. You hug them for me and tell them I love them, just as I love you. Remember that always."

And he rode away.

Walter, when he waked from his nap, was hurt and bewildered to find his father gone. "He didn't even tell me good-bye," he sobbed. Lillian was too young to understand, but she cried, too. Nothing his mother said soothed Walter's hurt.

Weeks later, Captain Stephen Cleveland came home on leave. Walter and Lillian, playing with their nurse under the shade of the cedars in the front yard, saw him coming down the drive and ran toward him.

But Walter stopped. He turned away as his father approached.

"What's the matter? Aren't you glad to see me?" Stephen asked.

"You went off without telling me good-bye," Walter replied.

Stephen reached down and pulled the boy close to him. "I'm sorry. I'll never do it again," he promised. "I'll always tell you good-bye."

So when the day arrived that Stephen had to leave to rejoin his company, he called Walter to him.

"I have to go," he told the boy. "You take care of your mama and little sister while I'm gone. I'll be back soon." He started down the steps and then he paused.

"Come on," he said to Walter. "There's time for us to take a quick ride before I go."

Holding the boy in front of him on his horse, Stephen galloped down the road, then turned back to the house and rode up the north steps, around the porch, and down the east steps.

"Do it again! Please do it again!" Walter shouted.

"I will. I'll do it the next time I come home. I promise. We'll have a fine ride around the porch, you and I. Now, good-bye." And Stephen was gone.

But there were no more of those wild, noisy rides around the porch for father and son. Walter died on a July day in 1861. He was almost five years old.

For a while, after the death of his son, Stephen was inconsolable. A grief so heavy that it seemed almost a physical burden pressed down upon on him, and there was no escape or surcease.

Perhaps it was an effort to overcome his crushing sorrow that prompted Stephen Cleveland to become involved in organizing a company of calvary soldiers for the Confederacy. It was easy enough to recruit members from among his friends in the Suggsville area, but he needed a larger number of horsemen for the outfit.

The September 12, 1861, issue of the *Clarke County Democrat* carried this notice on its editorial page: "We are requested by Captain Stephen B. Cleveland to state that there is still room for any persons desirous of joining his Cavalry Company.

"All who are not members of the Company may meet in Suggsville on Saturday next for that purpose—and should there be any who cannot get ready by that time, they will still be received by making early application.

"Captain Cleveland deserves great credit for the energy displayed in this truly important enterprise, and with his management and those who are aiding him, there is no doubt of success.

"Every young man now has an opportunity of doing something for his country. We hope all will come forward without delay who intend joining the company."

The next week's issue of the paper carried this news:

"Capt. S. B. Cleveland's Cavalry Company left Suggsville for Mobile on last Monday. It now consist of about 60 men, and as will be seen by a notice in another column, a few more recruits are wanted. This is an elegant company and those who can do so would do well to join it."

Mounted members of the Clarke County Ranger (the unit, sometimes referred to as The Suggsville Gray, later became a part of a regiment recruited by General Wirt Adams of Mississippi) gathered in the yard at the Cleveland home before their departure for Mobile. Captain Cleveland spoke to them briefly, thanking them for their display of patriotism, and then he got on his horse.

Instead of riding directly down the drive to the

road, he turned his mount sharply toward the house and rode at a gallop up the north steps, around the porch, and down the east steps.

Some people standing nearby (a large crowd had assembled to bid the company Godspeed) thought they heard him say, "Good-bye, Walter," but nobody was sure. It did seem to be a sort of farewell ritual, a good-bye to a home and to a way of life he loved. And perhaps it was part of a promise made to a beloved child.

Stephen Cleveland never stopped grieving over the death of his son. It was a grief he carried to his grave, for only at his own death in 1883 was his heart at peace.

The Cleveland house, built with such care, still stands in a wooded area near Suggsville. It is almost unchanged in appearance; even the porches and the steps are the same.

Now a private hunting club uses the house as a lodge. Often members say, the are awakened around midnight by the clatter of a horse's hoofs mounting the north steps, racing around the porch, and charging down the east steps. There is never a visible horse and rider, just the unmistakable sound of a horse being guided on a familiar route across the porch.

Hunters who hear the sound of the phantom rider say, "Listen. Do you hear that? It's Stephen Cleveland saying good-bye again to his little boy, keeping a promise he made a long, long, time ago."

4

The Curse of Barnsley Gardens

Near Rome, Georgia

*T*he scenery is beautiful, even more beautiful than you had described it to me, but please, can't we build our house on another location?" Julia Barnsley asked her husband.

"Why?" Godfrey Barnsley replied. It had never occurred to him that Julia would object to the site he had chosen for what he intended to be the finest house in all of Georgia.

"Why?" he asked again. "What is wrong with this location? It's perfect, right here on top of this knoll with the spring and the creek at the rear. And sweep-

ing down from the house will be our gardens stretch-
ing for acres and acres across the countryside. Why
don't you like this site?" he asked again, still puzzled.

"Look," he continued, not waiting for her reply,
"just let me show you what I have in mind. We'll build
the center section with its three-story tower here, and
then there'll be wings extending along the top of the
knoll, about here, with—"

Julia interrupted him. "The plans for the house are
perfect, but can't we put it somewhere else? Surely
there is another suitable hill in the 10,000 acres of land
you bought! I keep remembering what the people in
town said about this knoll having a curse on it. It
frightens me."

"Nonsense!" Barnsley retorted sharply. "Surely
you don't believe that foolish Indian superstition. I
am surprised and disappointed in you, Julia!" To
soften his words, for he seldom quarreled with his
wife, Barnsley reached out and took her hand.

"This knoll is the one right location for our house,
and I will build it here. We will call it Woodlands."

So Godfrey Barnsley, who had come from England some twenty years before and had become one

of Georgia's wealthiest men, began that summer of 1844 to build the architectural showplace that was to bring tragedy to everyone who lived in it—just as the Cherokee Indian superstition warned.

Barnsley moved his wife and children from Savannah, the city where he had amassed his fortune but where he considered the climate unhealthy. They crowded into a small house they were to occupy while the mansion was being built.

It was rather like camping out, and the children delighted in the adventure, but Julia was uneasy. Her feeling of foreboding increased as she watched her husband direct the felling of the trees on the knoll and as she saw him show the workman where to dig the foundations for Woodlands. She tried to be enthusiastic about the project, for she knew that Barnsley was building the house for her pleasure, but she kept hearing like a taunting echo, "There's a curse on the knoll—a curse—a curse —"

Barnsley was too busy planning and supervising the building of the grand mansion to be aware of his wife's increasing apprehension, and, after that first day at Woodlands when she had spilled out her fears to him, Julia never mentioned the topic again.

During the summer of 1845 Julia Barnsley became ill with what was diagnosed as a lung infection. Though she appeared for a while to be recovering, she died before the summer ended, and her infant son soon followed his mother in death. Thus Julia Scarborough Barnsley, age 34, and her baby were the first Barnsleys to fall victims to the "superstitious Indian curse."

The death of his beautiful young wife was a crushing sorrow to Godfrey Barnsley. For years, friends recall, he could not speak her name without weeping, and no woman ever replaced her in his love.

Soon after Julia's death, Barnsley took his children to New Orleans in a vain attempt to escape the memories of Julia that engulfed him so completely at Woodlands. After a time, when the acute grief had passed, Barnsley brought his family back to the north Georgia mountains. Work, he decided, would help him deal with his loneliness and grief, so he reassembled his workmen and ordered them to resume construction of Woodlands.

Barnsley devoted his entire attention to Woodlands. His money, his talents, his thoughts, and his strength were all directed toward one goal: Woodlands, the home and the gardens, must be a fitting memorial to his beloved Julia.

Progress was slow. Barnsley's requirement that every detail be perfect combined with the delay in receiving the marble mantels from Italy, the hand-fashioned paneling and the silver key plates from England, and the art treasures from throughout the world slowed the work.

A landscape architect, P. J. Berckman, came from Belgium to supervise the plantings of the formal gardens. The sweeping green lawns and terraces were centered with an oval maze of English boxwoods covering twenty acres, and along the divided drive and walkways were planted exotic trees: hemlocks and spruces from Norway, lindens, Japanese yews, firs, chestnuts, Scotch rowens. Grey boulders were hauled by ox team from the nearby mountains to provide the setting for the rock gardens.

As the gardens grew in beauty and scope, neighbors began referring to the place as Barnsley Gardens. In time the original name, Woodlands, was almost forgotten.

The house was not nearly finished in 1850 when Anna, the oldest daughter married T. C. Gilmour and moved to England. Work was still in progress in 1857 when the second daughter, Adelaide, married John K. Reid of New Orleans.

A year later when Adelaide came home to Woodlands to die, her father was still engrossed in the final phases of construction. Adelaide was buried beside her mother and her baby brother.

Once again Godfrey Barnsley had cause to recall the tale of the Indian curse.

The family had long ago moved from the small house where they first lived into a completed wing of the mansion. As various phases of construction were finished, the Barnsleys expanded the area of their living quarters.

It was soon after they moved into the big house that Barnsley confided to a friend, "Julia is here with me constantly. I see her walking in the garden, and her presence fills every room. Wherever I go at Woodlands, I feel her beside me."

When war came in 1861, the house was nearly completed. Only the handcarved stairway, which had been ordered from England, and the parquet floors remained to be installed.

Godfrey Barnsley was too old for military service, but his youngest sons, Lucian and George, joined the Confederate Army. A third son, Howard, the oldest, was in the Orient collecting plants and art treasures for Woodlands when the hostilities began. It was a mission from which he never returned. In 1862 Barnsley was notified that Howard had been killed by Chinese pirates.

Once again he wondered about the Indian curse.

It was in 1864 that Julia Barnsley, named for her mother, married Captain James P. Baltzelle, a provost marshall in the Confederate Army. Captain Baltzelle sent his bride to Savannah to refugee when Federal troops began moving toward Woodlands, and their daughter, Adelaide, was born in that port city.

The warning of the approach of the enemy was brought to Woodlands by Colonel Robert G. Earle, Second Alabama Cavalry. The Confederate officer rode through the formal gardens toward the house shouting,

"The Yankees are coming!"

A vanguard of the federal troops was almost on his heels, and before Colonel Earle could escape he was shot from his saddle by a private from Company A, 98th Illinois Volunteers.

And so there was another grave at Woodlands, another reminder of the Indian curse.

The burial was delayed, however, while the Federal troops ransacked the house in search of the gold and treasure they expected to capture there. When they failed to find gold and when the treasures they had anticipated turned out to be paintings, statuary, and rare books, the soldiers vented their disgust by breaking the statuary, slashing the paintings, snatching the books from the shelves, smashing the china and crystal and kicking holes in the woodwork.

Their most welcome prizes were found in the cellar where Godfrey Barnsley stored his Madeira wine, Scotch and brandies. The soldiers helped themselves.

Hours later Godfrey Barnsley stood on the front terrace and watched as the last of the invaders rode their horses through his rose garden and through his boxwood hedges. Then he turned and walked slowly into the ruins of his home, his Woodlands. "Julia—Julia," he sobbed in loneliness and frustration.

When he had recovered his composure and his strength, Barnsley made arrangements to bury his friend, Colonel Earle. The body was placed in a grave near the kitchen wing of the house, not far from where the soldier fell, and the spot was marked by a small stone from the hillside. Later the officer's name and rank were carved on the stone.

Soon after the War ended, members of Colonel Earle's family came from Alabama to move his body home, but by that time the story of the curse on Barnsley Gardens had become so widespread that they could find no one willing to help them exhume the body. They had no choice but to leave the grave undisturbed and to return to Alabama.

The war left Godfrey Barnsley penniless. His mansion had been vandalized, his gardens were a tangle of weeds and vines, and the cotton business in which he had amassed his fortune was gone.

Even his sons did not return to Woodlands. Rather than take the oath of allegiance to the United States, the brothers sailed for South America. They settled in

San Paulo, Brazil, where their descendants live until this day.

Barnsley left Woodlands, too. He moved to New Orleans where he had friends and where he intended to regain his lost fortune.

Into the shambles of Woodlands moved Julia and James Baltzelle and their little girl, Adelaide. Baltzelle hoped to support his family by selling timber from the Barnsley lands, but it was an ill-fated venture. In 1868 he was helping cut timber for shipment by rail from Hall's Station when he was struck and killed by a falling tree.

The curse of Barnsley Gardens had claimed another victim.

After the death of her husband, Julia fled from Woodlands and took her child to New Orleans to live with Barnsley. It was in New Orleans that she met and married a German sea captain named Charles H. von Schwartz.

Von Schwartz probably saw the fabled Barnsley Gardens for the first time in 1873 when Julia brought her father's body home for burial.

As the group of mourners turned to leave the

family burying ground, a neighbor observed, "Godfrey Barnsley is at peace now for the first time since his Julia died."

Nine-year-old Adelaide, or Addie as she was called, had accompanied her parents to the funeral. She looked at the massive house and the overgrown gardens, and she questioned and she wondered for no one had the patience or the perception to answer the questions that nagged at the mind of the child.

It would be years later, when she herself was mistress of Barnsley Gardens, that Addie would commune with the restless spirits of the dead and would understand the troubled feeling that crowded in upon her that day at her Grandfather Barnsley's funeral.

Addie was twenty-one when she came to Barnsley Gardens to stay. Her stepfather had died in 1885, and Addie and her mother, having nowhere else to go, came home to Barnsley Gardens.

As the two women hacked paths through the heavy undergrowth that had destroyed the symmetry of the gardens and as they worked together to make part of the old house livable, Julia talked with Addie about the grandeur of Woodlands as she remembered it from childhood. She told of the banquet table that seated forty guests, of Godfrey Barnsley's ingenious plan for providing running water in the bathrooms and kitchen by installing a cistern atop the tower in the center of the building, of the twenty-six-foot drawing room and the billiard room and the library with its leather-bound books.

Addie listened and tried to imagine how Barnsley Gardens looked in those years before the War. And when her mother wept over the departed glory, Addie comforted her by saying, "Don't cry, Mama. Just keep remembering how it used to be. We can restore it. I know we can."

Gradually, just as her grandfather had been obsessed with building Woodlands, Addie became obsessed with the determination to restore it.

Addie listened to other stories about Woodlands, too, stories that neighbors and former servants told about the Indian curse and about the tragedies that followed the building of Woodlands. She heard accounts of ghosts that roamed about the premises: her grandparents, Julia and Godfrey Barnsley, and the homesick spirit of Colonel Robert Earle.

She heard rumors, too, that her grandfather's body had been dug up by grave robbers who cut off his hand to use in pagan voodoo rites. Addie never repeated this rumor to her mother.

She never told her mother, either, when she herself began to see the ghosts at Barnsley Gardens. It was her grandmother, Julia Barnsley, whom Addie saw first, Julia walking about the scraggly boxwoods near the entrance of the house.

For as long as she lived at Barnsley Gardens, Addie continued to see her grandmother strolling around the grounds. She was aware, too, of the presence of a spirit, whom she recognized as Colonel Earle, wearing the grey uniform of the Confederacy.

Though she never saw him, Addie frequently heard in the late afternoon the scraping sound of her grandfather pushing his chair back from his desk in the library. The scraping of that chair had, years before, signaled the time for Godfrey Barnsley's pre-dinner toddy.

Addie heard, too, the laughter of the Barnsley children at play in a now-deserted wing of the house, and on some nights she was awakened by the noise of ghostly hammers wielded by invisible workmen trying to finish building Woodlands.

The presence of these ghosts served somehow to strengthen Addie's determination to restore her ancestral home. Her dream of restoring Barnsley Gardens was shared by the man she married, A. A. Saylor, a chemist. But though they talked and planned and assured each other that Barnsley Gardens would be elegant again, they never had sufficient money to get the project underway.

And the Indian curse lingered at Barnsley Gardens.

Saylor died, leaving Addie to rear their young children alone. Then in 1906 a tornado swept down on Barnsley Gardens, destroying the roof and doing other damage. Mrs. Saylor, Addie, salvaged what furniture she could and moved her family into the undamaged wing of the house where she was to live until her death.

Despite these misfortunes, Addie Saylor never relinquished her dream of rebuilding Barnsley Gardens. From the time her sons, Preston and Harry, were babies, Addie talked with them of the former majesty of Barnsley Gardens and urged them to spend their lives bringing beauty and order back to their family home. The boys were intrigued by the stories Addie told, and they promised solemnly, as children will, to work together to make their mother's dream a reality.

But they forgot the curse, and they never reckoned that they would be the principals in Barnsley Gardens' greatest tragedy.

As they grew older, the brothers became suspicious and envious of each other. Preston, having an adventurous and daring nature, became a professional boxer and achieved some success in the ring. Harry, after service with the infantry in World War I, returned to Barnsley Gardens to live with his mother. Harry's return revived Addie's waning hopes of having the needed work done at Barnsley Gardens.

Preston's boxing career ended when he suffered serious head injuries in a fight. Those injuries, friends said, affected his mind to such an extent that it became necessary to have him committed to the state hospital for the insane.

Preston blamed Harry for having him confined,

and he swore vengeance. In March, 1935, he escaped from the institution. Eight months later Preston appeared at Barnsley Gardens. He burst into the living room where Addie and Harry were talking (it was their favorite subject, the restoration of Barnsley Gardens that they were discussing), and he fired a single shot through Harry's heart.

Harry died in his mother's arms.

For seven more years Addie lived at Barnsley Gardens with her lost dreams. One son was dead, the other in prison. Now no one was left who loved Barnsley Gardens as she did or who wanted to make it beautiful again. Roofless walls crumbled, arches collapsed, trees grew through rotted flooring, vines crept through the broken windows.

In her lonely quarters, Addie Saylor watched the ghost of her grandmother stroll in the garden. She heard her grandfather scrape his chair across the floor in the library and heard the Barnsley children laugh and heard the pounding of phantom hammers. She met the restless spirit of Colonel Earle when she went to get water from the spring back of the house. They were, all of them, welcome, familiar companions.

Another apparition appeared. Harry's spirit came back to talk with his mother, to ask,

"Mama, is there really a curse on Barnsley Gardens? Is that why we've been plagued by tragedy? Is there really a curse here?"

And Addie remembered the story she had heard of a young woman named Julia Barnsley who begged her husband, "Please, can't we build our house on another location?"

5

The Ghost Collie at Scataway

SCATAWAY, GEORGIA

They tell strange tales up in the mountains of north Georgia, up around Owl Town and Shake Rag and Lower Tater Ridge, tales of monsters and witches and boogers and other embodiments of evil, but it is the story of the white collie, a gentle and pathetic dog, that is told most often at Scataway.

Some people now living in the Scataway community that sprawls along the mountain valley have seen the ghost collie and can give personal testimony of these encounters. Other stories of the phantom dog begin, "My grandpa used to tell me—," or, "Mama's oldest sister, Aunt Vonnie, said she—." The accounts, though they vary in detail, all relate the story of a white collie that used to return from the dead to search for his owner in Scataway.

Perhaps no one tells the story of the sorrowing animal better than does Hugh Oliver. Hugh Oliver left his rugged, unspoiled hills to find adventure in far countries, and he has now returned to claim fulfillment at a place called Bald Mountain Park.

"I saw the ghost dog," Hugh Oliver says, "and I patted him. And he licked my hand. It's been more than forty years ago, but I can still remember how his fur felt, and I can still feel his tongue licking my hand."

HUGH WAS ABOUT EIGHT YEARS OLD when it happened, and he was visiting his older sister at Scataway. The sister was named Blon, Miss Blon Oliver, and she was the teacher at the one-room Scataway school.

School zones were vague, and enforcement of attendance laws was lax in those days, so sometimes when Miss Blon came home for the weekend, Hugh would go back to Scataway with her and attend school for a week or two.

Miss Blon boarded with Mr. and Mrs. Silas Deaton, an elderly couple who lived about a quarter of a mile from the frame schoolhouse. Nearly everybody in Scataway, even people not kin to them, called the couple Grandma and Grandpa Deaton, sort of titles of affection and respect.

The Deatons' house was right close to the main road that came through the gap and ran through the valley. It was not a big house, but it was comfortable and Miss Blon liked boarding there. She had a small bedroom that opened off the front room, the main room in the house. Her furniture was plain: a feather bed, a straight chair and a table (both handmade) to hold her books, a washstand with a bowl and pitcher. The floor was bare, its wide boards worn smooth by many feet and many scrubbings. The room's only decorations were an oval picture of a nameless Deaton ancestor in a flat frame, a cross-stitched sampler with colored X's spelling out "The Lord Is My Shepherd," and a calendar with a picture of a lighthouse on it.

Miss Blon had promised to save the picture for Hugh when the year ended.

Grandma and Grandpa Deaton liked to have Hugh come to visit them. When she knew he was coming, Grandma Deaton would make teacakes and have them tied in a clean flour sack in the corner of the kitchen safe. Hugh knew where to find them.

Grandpa Deaton would show Hugh how to whittle an airplane, complete with a propeller that really twirled, though neither of them had ever seen an airplane close up. Grandpa Deaton also carved tiny baskets out of peach seeds, and they made whang-doodles and tops, too. Once Grandpa Deaton whittled out a wooden chain with thirteen links, but he would not give it to Hugh until the boy could name the thirteen colonies. It was a history lesson Hugh never forgot.

Miss Blon enjoyed Hugh's visits, too. "Hugh's a help to me," she would tell their parents when Hugh asked permission to go over to Scataway with her.

Hugh did try to help. He carried Miss Blon's books and their lunch pail when they walked to school in the early mornings. In the wintertime he took out the ashes and helped build a fire in the iron stove that heated the schoolroom. After he had warmed his hands and his feet, Hugh would take the water bucket from the shelf near the window and go to the well to get fresh drinking water for the day.

He never volunteered to help Miss Blon with the sweeping, but occasionally after school, after all the other children had left, Hugh would volunteer to wash the blackboard. He did not want any of the boys to see him doing what he considered to be girls' work.

Though Hugh Oliver has many tales to tell of his childhood visits to Scataway, his strangest story is of the night the ghost collie came.

It had been a night like many other nights. They had eaten supper in the kitchen close to the wood range, and after supper Hugh had brought in an armload of logs for the big fireplace in the front room. He had sat on a braided rug, one Grandma Deaton had made, in front of the fire and had listened to Grandpa Deaton tell tales of his boyhood. Miss Blon was grading papers, and Grandma Deaton was picking out hickory nuts.

Hugh was sleepy. He had gotten up early to go to

school with his sister, and he had played many games of whoopy-hide at recess, at noontime and after school. Now the warmth of the fire and the soothing rhythm of Grandpa Deaton's voice made him drowsy.

He was glad when Miss Blon put her schoolwork away and said, "Well, Hugh, it's time we went to bed." Hugh undressed quickly and stood warming by the fire while Grandpa Deaton read a chapter from the Bible. Then he gave the adults a good-night hug and ran to bed.

The stack of quilts—bear paw, Jacob's ladder, star, all pieced by Grandma Deaton—felt good. He was nearly asleep when Miss Blon reached beneath the covers and wrapped his feet in a wool sweater she had warmed by the fire. He was asleep when Miss Blon made sure the window was tightly closed, buttoned the door, and crawled into bed beside him.

The next thing Hugh knew he was wide awake. It was near dawn but sunrise was still a promise, and the room held the greyness of fading night. At first Hugh could not decide what had waked him. Miss Blon was still asleep, and there was no sound of Grandma and Grandpa Deaton stirring. Some noise had aroused him though, some unusual noise. Hugh lay still and listened.

He heard it again, the noise that had called him from sleep, quite distinctly this time: he heard the scratchy padding of a dog's feet across the bare floor. Then he heard panting, the way a dog does when he has run a long way.

Hugh looked over the edge of the bed, and there sitting on his haunches and looking right at him was a dog, a big white collie. The boy instinctively reached out to pat the dog, to run his fingers through his fur. The dog licked Hugh's hand.

Suddenly Hugh felt uneasy. Something was wrong. Grandma and Grandpa Deaton did not have a dog; in all his visits to Scataway he had never seen a dog at their home. And how had the animal gotten into the room? The window was still closed, the door buttoned.

Hugh was frightened. "Blon! Blon!" he called as he shook his sister's shoulder. "Blon!"

"What is it, Hugh? What's wrong?" Blon asked sleepily. Then seeing the look on his face she said,

"You saw the dog, didn't you? The white collie."

"Yes—but how did you know?" Hugh replied "How could you know?"

"He comes often, and—"

"He's here now," Hugh interrupted, "right by the bed."

But when he looked, the dog was gone.

The window was still closed; the door still buttoned. There had been no sound, no clicking of claws on the bare floor, but the white collie was gone.

"Don't be frightened," Miss Blon said, gathering Hugh in her arms. "It's all right. I can't explain it. All I know is that he's a ghost dog that comes here every now and then. Grandpa Deaton says he's looking for somebody. He's friendly but kind of sad. Don't be upset—it's all right," she said again.

They could hear Grandpa Deaton moving around then, could hear the clatter of the metal eyes as he started a fire in the kitchen stove and could hear him stirring up coals and adding kindling to coax a blaze in the front room fireplace.

Hugh wondered if Grandpa Deaton had seen the dog, too.

"Come on—let's get dressed," Miss Blon urged.

"You can go dress in the front room by the fire."

"He licked my hand. That dog licked my hand right here," Hugh said, holding out his hand to his sister.

Miss Blon held Hugh's hand and looked first at the spot he showed her and then deep into his eyes. "Here," she said, handing him a wet washrag, "Wash your face and hands for breakfast."

Hugh was not hungry. He sat at the table, but he could not eat breakfast. He could not even drink the hot chocolate Grandma Deaton had fixed for him.

"What's wrong, boy? You sick?" Grandpa Deaton asked.

"He saw the dog, the white collie," Miss Blon explained. "He saw the dog, and it upset him."

"Come here, boy," Grandpa Deaton said. He took Hugh's hand and led him into the front room. Then he sat in front of the fire and held Hugh on his knees while he told the story of the white collie.

"A long time ago, back when there weren't many people or many houses in this valley, a man and his wife lived right here in this house. Nobody seems to know for sure what their names were. Maybe they were named Henson. That's a good name.

"Travelers coming through the valley would often stop here to spend the night. Mrs. Henson would cook them a good supper, and Mr. Henson would help see after their horse or their mule. Some folks didn't have a horse or a mule—they'd come walking in with a pack of stuff on their back.

"Sometimes the travelers would sleep in the room where Miss Blon sleeps now. If it was winter and cold or if there were a good many travelers here the same night, they might sleep here on the floor in front of the fire.

"Well, one time a man stopped here—he'd been before, maybe half a dozen times—and he told Mrs. Henson, 'I've brought you a surprise.' And he reached inside his coat and he brought out the cutest little fuzzy puppy you ever did see. Solid white. Just a ball of white fur.

"The puppy looked so much like a snowball, that's what they started to name it, but Mrs. Henson said that was too common a name. She wanted her dog to have a special name, not like every other white dog was named, so she named him Frost. Frost can be mighty white and thick too, you know.

"Frost kinda got to be a pet with everybody. He grew to be a big, friendly dog, and he liked just about everybody, but it seemed like he knew he was Mrs. Henson's dog, and he really loved that woman. He'd follow her around, and he's lie down close to her when she was working in the kitchen—not get in the way, you know, just be close.

"Folks who stopped often at the Henson's house got real fond of Frost, and some of them even gave him presents. The cobbler made Frost a leather collar, all hand-tooled and decorated, while he was in the community mending shoes, and a tinker made Frost a big tin bowl with his name across the rim. Hunters were all the time bringing Frost big bones to gnaw on.

"Well, late one winter afternoon this man came riding up and asked if he could spend the night. Mr. Henson went to the door when the man knocked. He didn't like the fellow's looks and would have turned him away, but the weather was uncommonly cold and cloudy and looking like snow, and Mr. Henson hated to send anybody out in a mountain storm.

"So he told the man he could come on in and

spend the night—if he didn't mind sleeping in front of the fire. You see, Mr. Henson knew Mrs. Henson wasn't going to let anybody dirty as that stranger sleep in her good bed.

"Frost didn't like the stranger at all. Soon as the man walked into the front room, Frost commenced to growl real low and to move up close to Mrs. Henson. Mrs. Henson tried to calm the dog, but it was plain that Frost didn't want the man in the house.

"Well. Frost got so riled up that Mr. Henson finally shut him up in the bedroom so Mrs. Henson could fix supper, but Frost scratched on the door and barked and cut up so bad they had to let him out.

"Mrs. Henson held Frost by the collar and kept saying she was sorry for the way the dog was acting and telling the man that Frost never had bitten anybody, but you could tell that the man didn't like Frost any better than Frost liked him. He was scared of Frost, too.

"Now, nobody knows exactly what happened later on that night.

"Next afternoon, somebody passing the house stopped to speak to the Hensons. The visitor called a couple of times but nobody answered, and he whistled for Frost, but Frost didn't come.

"The man felt like something was wrong, so he went to get some help. Some men working down the road came with him and broke open the door, and they found Mr. and Mrs. Henson dead. Murdered. Frost was dead, too. He was lying right at Mrs. Henson, like he might have been trying to protect her.

"Folks figured that the stranger, whoever he was, must have thought the Hensons had some money hid at their house, and he aimed to rob them. It was a bad thing. Real bad.

"The house stayed empty a long time after that. Nobody wanted to live in it. Then finally some new people moved in, folks who didn't know anything about what had happened to the Hensons.

"They'd been living there a good while when the man asked somebody after preaching one Sunday if he knew anything about a white collie. Said they kept seeing the dog around the place. Said the dog would just come from nowhere—just come—and then he'd disappear the same way. Said the dog never would eat anything, that he'd just walk through the house like he was looking for somebody he knew and missed.

"The way he described the dog, the collar and all, folks at church knew it was Frost. Couldn't have been any other dog.

"We, Grandma and I, been living here a long time now, and ever since we've been here, we've been seeing that dog, Frost. Sometimes we'll be sitting before the fire here in the front room, and we'll look and there'll be a big white dog sitting on his haunches right there between us. He'll sit there and look at the fire. Won't lie down, just sit there. Then he'll walk around like he's hoping to find somebody. Then he'll go away.

"So that's the dog you saw in Miss Blon's room this morning, that's the ghost collie. He's still looking for his mistress."

"I CAN STILL REMEMBER HOW his fur felt when I petted him. And I can still feel his tongue licking my hand," Hugh Oliver says.

6

The Light in the Graveyard
ST. SIMONS ISLAND, GEORGIA

*S*t. Simons Island is so rich in ghost lore that natives there seldom agree on which of the many supernatural happenings is the most outstanding.

Some of the islanders favor the story of Mary the Wanderer (or Mary de Wanda), the grieving woman who meanders along deserted roadways searching for her drowned lover.

Other residents of St. Simons like best the ghost of a lightkeeper who for years haunted the tall white lighthouse on the tip of the island. His heavy footsteps on the spiral stairway were familiar sounds to the men working in the tower, and their families who lived in the cottage adjoining the lighthouse accepted the clatter of the restless feet as a natural supplement to their household noises.

Then there are the stories of the shipload of captives from the African Ibo tribe who walked into the sea rather than spend their lives in slavery and whose doleful chant, "The water brought us, the water will take us away," is still heard around the mouth of Dunbar Creek, and of Flora de Cookpot whose delectable, calorie-filled foods can be smelled simmering on an invisible stove, and of the tormented ghost of a former owner of Kelvyn Grove Plantation who roams the grounds seeking his murderer.

But the most often told and certainly the most appealing ghost story on the island is the account of the light in the graveyard at Christ Church, Frederika.

Nobody remembers her full name, but all residents of St. Simons know the story of the young woman whose fear of the dark prompted her husband, after her death, to put a lighted candle on her grave each night for as long as he lived.

According to the story, Emma, on whose grave the candle glows, had always been afraid of the dark. Her mother traced the fear back to an old nurse who whispered terrifying tales of witches and vampires and voodoo and evil spirits to the child "to make her behave." The nurse was assigned other, and decidedly less pleasant duties when it became known that she was deliberately frightening Emma, but by then the damage had been done.

Emma's father, who loved his only daughter deeply and who usually indulged her every whim, took her fears lightly at first.

"There's nothing to be afraid of," he assured her. "Forget all those false tales. Nothing is going to hurt you. Not ever."

Though reason and reassurance seemed to be effective in dealing with the child's fears in the daytime, when night came the dread of the dark possessed her again. She screamed in fright if she was left alone in the dark for even a few minutes.

Her mother tried to soothe Emma by reminding her of God's care and by teaching her a poem about the dark which began,

"The dark is soft and gentle.

"The dark is kind and sweet.

"The dark will pat my pillow

"And love me as I sleep."

Neither the reminder nor the poetry was effective.

Then Emma's father lost patience with what he termed her "senseless, spoiled display of fear."

"Put Emma to bed as usual," he instructed her new nurse. "Make sure she is comfortable, and then put out the lamp, close the door, and leave her alone. She is quite old enough to remain in a darkened room by herself, and she must not be indulged in this childishness any longer!"

The nurse reluctantly did as she was told, but as soon as she had put out the lamp and closed the door, she hurried from the house and walked down a winding plantation road for nearly half a mile until she could no longer hear Emma's screams.

Emma's father steeled himself against entering her room, and he forbade any other member of the household to respond to her pleas for light. Finally though, it was her father himself who went in to her. He had intended to be firm and to order her to stop creating such a furor, but when he saw that she was hysterical with fear, and when she collapsed in his arms, he gently placed her in bed, lighted a candle, and lay beside her until she fell asleep. He left the candle burning by her bed when he tiptoed from the room.

The next day he retracted the orders he had given the nurse, and he instructed her never to leave Emma alone in the dark but to make sure that a lighted candle, a fresh candle each night, was left beside her bed.

Even then her parents believed that in time Emma would outgrow her fear of the dark, but as the years passed the young girl became increasingly dependent on the security which the burning candle gave her.

She developed a distressing anxiety about running out of candles, and she began hoarding stubs which she collected from candlesticks around the house. She hid the stubs in her bureau drawer until her mother discovered them and was about to throw them away (one of them had melted and had matted the lace and tatting on a nearly new chemise).

Emma begged so pitifully to be allowed to keep the pieces of candles that her mother agreed to let her put them in a box in the corner of the pantry.

Except for this fear of the dark, Emma was a normal, happy, attractive girl. She had many friends, and her invitations to parties and to outings kept her social calendar filled. When they were younger, her friends sometimes teased her about being afraid of the dark, but in time they accepted it as being as natural as the fears some of them had of snakes or of water or even of horses. A few of the girls even considered Emma's nightly candle a bit romantic and wished that their parents would allow them to cultivate such a dramatic idiosyncrasy.

As for the boys, knowledge of Emma's fear of darkness aroused their protective instincts, and she was never lacking for escorts dedicated to guarding her from whatever dangers might lurk in the shadows.

It was at a houseparty in Brunswick that Emma met the young man, Phillip, whom she was later to marry. He had recently moved to Brunswick from the Carolinas to join a cotton brokerage firm, so he knew nothing of Emma's terror of darkness.

He only knew that he loved her.

Emma, of course, was aware of Phillip's love, but she did not feel that she could or should encourage it until he knew about her abnormal reaction to darkness. Yet she could not bring herself to tell him about it. For the first time in her life Emma was truly embarrassed to talk of her fear. It seemed so childish, so beneath the dignity of a woman old enough to be thinking of marriage. Night after night she worried about telling him of her "affliction," staying awake until her candle burned low in its holder.

On the night, several months after they had met, that Phillip asked her to become his wife, she knew she could no longer delay the revelation.

"There is something I must tell you," she began. Already her voice was shaking and she was near tears. "I cannot accept your proposal of marriage—I do love you, Phillip—until I am completely honest with you about my background. You see—"

Phillip was stunned. What did she have in her past that would upset her so? Had there been an unfortunate love affair? Did she have a dread malady? Surely she was not in love with someone else!

"What is it, Emma? What is it? Tell me. Nothing

can change my love for you. Nothing!"

"It's—oh, Phillip, I'm afraid of the dark!" Emma blurted out.

"Afraid of the dark! Is that all?" Phillip laughed with relief.

"Don't laugh, Phillip. Please don't. It's awful, this fear of mine." The tears came.

Phillip wiped her eyes with his handkerchief, and then cupping her hands in his, he said, "Emma, you must not cry. And you must not be afraid. Not ever. Not of anything. I will take care of you. Always."

They were married, Emma and Phillip, at Christ Church, Frederika, and afterwards they stood in the shade of the massive oaks outside the church, the same oaks beneath which Charles and John Wesley had preached more then a century before, to receive the good wishes of their friends.

Phillip had taken Emma's confession of her fear of the dark rather lightly, but in time he learned to sleep quite well with a candle burning all night in their bedroom. Except for this adjustment, Emma and Phillip were completely happy together. They moved, after several months, from Brunswick to Frederika on

St. Simons Island where Phillip helped his father-in-law with managing his plantation and his shipping interests.

It was not long after this move that Phillip observed that Emma was becoming overly concerned about her supply of candles. She went to her childhood home and got the old box of candle stubs from the pantry, melted them down, and made new candles.

Then she busied herself making candles of beeswax. She explained to Phillip that the candles of beeswax burned more evenly and cast a more pleasant light than did candles molded of tallow.

By this time Emma had learned to estimate with amazing accuracy how long a candle would burn, and she made her candles different lengths to conform with the difference in the lengths of the nights. For example, candles intended for use in June were shorter than those to be used in December since June nights are shorter then December nights. She separated her candles by lengths, wrapped them in bundles, and labeled each bundle with the name of the month in which the candles were to be used. She then stored them in a cool basement closet.

She spent more and more time making candles, though she never let her candle-making interfere with her household duties or with her service to the church (she provided candles, taking them from her own precious store, for use in the sanctuary each Sunday, and she also taught a Sunday School class and was a leader in missionary work).

When Phillip, with the utmost patience, pointed out to Emma that she had enough candles to last for several years, and when he suggested that she devote her time to other, more pleasant activities, she replied,

"But the dark is so dreadful. I cannot bear it if I do not have the security of knowing I have many candles to protect me. Please understand, Phillip."

Though he did not really understand, Phillip humored her and continued to provide her with the growing amounts of wax and wicks she required. He loved her very much, and his concern for her obsession with candle-making only deepened that love.

Emma was making candles one afternoon when she spilled some of the hot wax on her arm, inflicting a deep and painful burn. She used the usual home remedies, but the injury did not heal properly. Infection set in and, despite the best efforts of doctors brought in by Phillip, blood poisoning developed.

Less then a week after the accident, Emma died.

She had realized the seriousness of her condition, and she talked calmly of death. "I am quite ready to die if it is God's will," she told the rector when he came to visit her.

But to Phillip she said, "It will be so dark, so very dark—"

Phillip leaned close to her and whispered, "You'll always have a light. Always."

After the funeral, in the late twilight of that long day, Phillip got a candle from the supply Emma had made and walked to her grave beside Christ Church. He pushed the candle into the soft dirt and lighted it.

"Here's your candle, my darling," he said. Then he turned quickly and went back to his empty house.

Every night for as long as he lived Phillip made this solitary trek to the graveyard to place a candle on Emma's grave. When the weather was rainy or windy, he put the candle inside a small lantern fashioned of glass and tin so that the flame would not go out, but the weather was never too bad nor was business ever too pressing to prevent his performance of this nightly ritual.

Neighbors remarked on his faithfulness, and they explained the significance of the burning candle to strangers who inquired.

When Phillip died, he was buried beside Emma at Christ Church.

For several nights after Phillip's death, people passing the graveyard saw the familiar light on Emma's grave. They were surprised at first, but they decided that some of the neighbors were carrying on Phillip's custom of placing a candle there.

However, inquiry disclosed that no one on the island was responsible for the light, no one was taking candles to the grave. The source of the burning taper was—and still is—a mystery.

In the years that have followed, hundreds of people on St. Simons have seen the patch of light like the soft glow of a candle on a time-weathered grave at Christ Church.

The brick wall around the church property hides the graves from the road now so that the light is not seen by motorists driving past the burial spot. However, people who walk down the road beneath the moss-hung limbs of the old oaks or who pause to lean against the brick wall and stare at the graves still tell occasionally of seeing a peculiar, flickering light.

These sightings prompt the re-telling of the story of the young woman who was afraid of the dark and her devoted husband who promised, "You'll always have a light. Always."

7

Nellie

Columbus, Mississippi

S itting on the front porch of the old Weaver home and rocking and listening to Miss Nellie talk was as fine a history lesson about Columbus as anybody could have.

Miss Nellie knew everything there was to know about that old river town. She knew about the buildings, and she knew about the people whose lives were a part of those buildings.

She also knew nearly everybody who passed along the sidewalk in front of her house, and she interrupted her rocking and her talking to speak to them and to inquire about members of their families. Each passerby stirred another of Miss Nellie's cubbyholes of memories and prompted the telling of another chapter in the chronicles of Columbus.

As she grew older—she lived to be eighty—Miss Nellie spent more and more time in her rocking chair on the front porch. Looking out across the boxwood hedge and the iron fence (both there before she was born) with her back to the cracked windows and the broken shutters and the dingy walls, she could forget for a little while that her house was worn and shabby.

The house seemed to have gone down—that was a term her father would have used—so quickly that she was overwhelmed by the magnitude of the repairs it needed. Yet she knew that was not true: the changes had come gradually. Time and neglect, not willful neglect but neglect nevertheless, had taken their relentless toll.

She remembered walking through the back parlor one afternoon (was it last year? five years ago? ten?) and glanced into the tall mirror. A stranger, wrinkled and disheveled, stared back at her.

For the first time, Miss Nellie knew that she was old.

Having seen the changes in herself, she looked

closely at her house. It, too, had changed: the graceful elegance of the familiar rooms, rooms where she had spent her entire life, had been swallowed up by deterioration and drabness. Going from room to room, Miss Nellie, felt like an intruder, as though she had mistakenly come to the wrong address.

"Well," she said aloud, "we've gotten old, this house and I. Not long ago, this was the loveliest house, and I was the prettiest girl in Columbus. But we're quality—we'll survive."

It was true, her observation about the loveliness of the house and her beauty.

The house had been built by her father, William B. Weaver, a Columbus merchant, in 1848. That was in the prosperous pre-War days when there was money and labor to indulge the tastes of cultured men such as William Weaver for residences of classic elegance.

Select lumber was shipped up the Tombigbee River from Mobile. Marble mantles were imported from Italy. The front of the house had an Italianate influence with its delicate arches of wooden tracery connecting the six octagonal columns. The columns were decorated with plaster medallions of acanthus leave, and flawless pier mirrors reflected the lights from chandeliers into infinity.

It was a lovely house, a perfect setting for a girl as vivacious and as pretty as Nellie Weaver.

Many of the tales Miss Nellie, an older Miss Nellie, told as she rocked on the porch of the old Weaver home were of growing up in that house, of her childhood in Columbus. Her lifetime spanned the years from before the War between the States to the time of Great Depression in the 1930s, and her recollections from each period were sharp and delightfully unique.

She told of the night back in 1863—she was eight years old then—when Confederate President Jefferson Davis, who was visiting Columbus, was awakened by hundreds of voices singing beneath his bedroom window. The townspeople had gathered to serenade their President with Southern airs. President Davis threw a robe over his long nightshirt and came out on a balcony to applaud the music and to make a little speech to the crowd.

"He was visiting in the James Whitefield house—it's the Billups house now—had come to attend a session of the Mississippi Legislature, I think. The capital had been moved here from Jackson. Jefferson Davis wasn't always popular, not even in his native Mississippi, but that night when he stood out there on the balcony with his hair all tousled and his nightshirt flapping around his ankles, the people in Columbus loved him."

She told, too, of the April day in 1866 when the ladies of Columbus (Miss Nellie had not quite attained the status of ladyhood, being only eleven, but she was not one to miss any momentous occasion) marched in a dignified procession to Friendship Cemetery to decorate the graves of the soldiers, Confederate and Union, with fresh flowers from their gardens. It was the first Memorial Day. Miss Nellie remembered how the flowers smelled, the wilted tulle bows that bound some of the bouquets, the sad sameness of the hundreds of earth mounds, and the reluctance of a few of the ladies to put their flowers on Union graves.

When she was older, Miss Nellie attended Columbus Female Institute, and in later years she was frequently called on to supply historic data about this private academy which was, a century and more later, to become Mississippi University for Women.

Growing up during Reconstruction, a time of depression and of re-adjustment, Miss Nellie learned early to adapt to loss and to change. Never in her long life did deprivations or inconvenience dull her keen delight in the wonder of life: for her, every day was a new adventure.

Miss Nellie could make a walk to the Post Office seem as exciting as a New Year's Eve ball. And if a garment needed mending, she could embroider a patch on it and wear it with such verve that every fashionable young lady in Columbus yearned for patches, too.

She had a talent for acting, and she often appeared in amateur theatricals in Columbus. Her portrayal of Lucy in Sheridan's *The Rivals* evoked prolonged applause from the audience at the old Gilmer House, and there were many comments to the effect that "that pretty Weaver girl is wasting her talents here in Columbus." There might have been suggestions that she appear on the New York stage, but the life of a professional actress was not quite acceptable in 1875, not for a Southern lady.

Yellowed clippings tell of her successes in the plays and of her popularity at dances and balls. "N. W. was the belle of the Mardi Gras ball," the Columbus society columns reported, printing an observation that everyone at the ball already knew.

Naturally, many young men came calling at the Weaver home. Miss Nellie enjoyed their company, was pleased with their attention, and graciously accepted their invitations to parties, picnics, boat rides, concerts, dances, parades, and church suppers. She liked them all; no one in particular; all of them.

Then Charles Tucker came to Columbus.

Their meeting was as exciting and as romantic as if it had been written for a story book.

Miss Nellie first saw Charles Tucker—she did not know his name—as he was helping to fight a fierce fire. Probably, like Miss Nellie, he had been attracted to the scene of the fire by curiosity. Once there, he saw that the fire-fighters needed help, so he handed his coat and hat to a stranger and joined in battling the blazes.

That is how Miss Nellie first saw Charles Tucker: his face flushed and streaked with soot, his shirt grimy and wet, his hair wild and disarrayed. In her eyes, he was a dashing hero.

"Who is he?" she asked. "Who is he? He's so handsome! Who is he?"

She must have asked two dozen people before someone told her, "His name is Charles Tucker, and he came from Virginia, Fredericksburg, I think."

Miss Nellie was in love, happily, deliriously, completely in love. She and Charles R. Tucker were married in the First Presbyterian Church in Columbus at 8:30 o'clock on the evening of February 28, 1878.

It may have been about then, either just before or just after she and Charles were married, that Nellie walked into the double parlor at the Weaver house one day and, using her diamond ring, etched NELLIE on a windowpane.

"Now I'll never be forgotten in this house: there will always be this reminder of me here. Always." She stood back and looked at her name on the pane and laughed with delight.

The name stayed on the pane, but the laughter vanished. At least for awhile. Charles and Nellie, they of the storybook romance, did not live happily ever after. They parted, and Miss Nellie reared their daughter, Ellen, in the same big house where she had grown up. Years later the grandchildren (Nell, Lulah, and the twins, Blanchard and Walter) came to the Weaver home.

For years Miss Nellie taught a private school at her home, earning the money she needed for her livelihood. She converted one of the servants' houses, long empty, in the back yard into a classroom. There she taught the children and the grandchildren of her friends.

Perhaps it was because of her preoccupation with her school and with her grandchildren that Miss Nellie did not notice how disreputable the Weaver place had become. By the time she became aware of it, she had neither the finances nor the energy to restore it.

About this time, about the time she faced and accepted the ravages of time, Miss Nellie's friends intensified their efforts to persuade her to move from the Weaver place into a small apartment or rooms where she would be more comfortable. At first, Miss Nellie was shocked at their suggestions. Later she became annoyed and stubbornly defensive.

"Leave my home? Never! It needs me, and my grandchildren need me. And I need them. I'll stay right here," she retorted. "Right here." Often she added, "Some day this house will be restored to the beautiful place it once was. You'll see. It will be lovely again."

So Miss Nellie stayed.

She rocked on her porch, and she told stories about the Columbus she loved, and she pretended not to notice that she and her house were both wearing out.

One night Miss Nellie's clothing caught fire from the open fireplace in the back parlor. She died as a result of the burns.

After her death, the Weaver house suffered further at the hands of destructive tenants, and vandals added their indignities to the structure.

Then about 1950, Mrs. Erroldine Hay Bateman bought the property and began its restoration. Her task seemed almost hopeless, but she saw beyond the dingy banners of peeling wallpaper, the cheap partitions that changed grand rooms into makeshift apartments, the leaky roof, and the rotting floors. Mrs.

Bateman saw the enduring beauty that William Weaver had built into his house, and she set about to reclaim it.

Mrs. Bateman named the house Errolton.

One day as she and her son, Douglas Bateman, were supervising some basic repairs in the double parlor, they happened to see the windowpane on which Miss Nellie had scratched her name years earlier. Most of the windows has been broken, but the pane with NELLIE on it remained intact.

"We must save that pane," Mrs. Bateman said. "It will be a touching reminder of Miss Nellie and her life in this house."

Unfortunately, a careless workman broke the pane. There was no way to salvage the pieces, so a new pane of glass had to be put in the window.

As the restoration progressed, Errolton became as beautiful as Mrs. Bateman had known it would be. The house seemed to come alive, almost as though it were resurrected, in response to the love and attention given it.

The restoration was nearly finished by the mid-1950s when Mr. and Mrs. Douglas Bateman moved into Errolton. She completed work in the upstairs bedrooms and added her inheritance of fine pieces of furniture to the house.

One afternoon not many years ago, Mrs. Douglas Bateman was walking through the back parlor when she noticed that the sun was shining through the window and was striking a sofa she had recently upholstered in blue. She did not want the sunlight to fade her sofa, so she went over to the window to pull the shade down.

As she reached for the shade, Mrs. Bateman noticed what appeared to be dust on the windowpane. She ran her hand across it, and the glass felt rough. Stepping back, she looked at the pane and saw etched there the word NELLIE. The word occupied the same position on the pane and in the window as the autographed pane that had be destroyed by the careless workman.

The Batemans think Miss Nellie came back and scratched her name on the windowpane to thank them for making her house lovely again. They call it "Miss Nellie's Window."

8

The Long, Long Visit
DUNLEITH, MISSISSIPPI

*H*ow long is she going to stay?" Sarah whispered to her mother. Mrs. Dahlgren gave her young daughter a reproving look. Then on the pretext of going out of the parlor to inquire about the progress of supper, she motioned Sarah to follow her.

Out in the hall, out of earshot of the guest, Mrs. Dahlgren said softly but firmly, "Miss Percy will stay here at Dunleith as long as she likes. She is your kinswoman, Sarah, your cousin, and I expect you to show her every consideration and courtesy, both as kinswoman and as guest."

"But why did . . .?" Sarah started to ask.

Mrs. Dahlgren cut her short. "That is all," she said. "There will be no more questions about Miss Percy. None. Do you understand?"

Two of Sarah's younger brothers, rowdy and out-spoken like their father, raced through the parlor and out into the hall.

"She talks funny," giggled one boy.

"She smells funny," added his brother.

Before their mother could rebuke them, they had run from the hall out onto the porch where they tussled and wrestled its columned length before tumbling over the grillwork bannister onto the lawn.

Mrs. Dahlgren replaced her frown of disapproval with what she hoped was a look of composure (composure is not easy to achieve in a household with eleven children) before she returned to the parlor.

If Miss Percy had overheard the remarks in the hall, she gave no evidence of it. She had risen from the sofa and was standing across the room beside a harp.

"Who plays this harp?" she asked, running her fingers across the strings.

She did talk "funny"; her native Mississippi drawl had a decided foreign accent, and her "funny smell" was the aroma of exotic perfume.

"Nobody plays the harp now. At least not often," Mrs. Dahlgren replied. "Mr. Dahlgren bought it for Sarah soon after we built Dunleith, hoping it would encourage her musical talents. She took lessons and learned to play rather well, but she never enjoyed the harp, and now she appears to have lost interest in it entirely."

"May I play?" Miss Percy asked.

"Please do!" Mrs. Dahlgren answered.

Miss Percy seated herself in a brocaded chair and drew the harp to her. She plucked the strings hesitantly at first, almost as though she feared a discordant rebuff from the instrument, but after a few minutes she began playing a rippling, sweet melody.

Mrs. Dahlgren did not recognize the tune, yet it seemed as familiar as lullabies she hummed to her children. As she listened, Mrs. Dahlgren decided that Miss Percy had composed the music as she played, drawing from the strings a song of love, of rejection, of homesickness, of loneliness.

Mrs. Dahlgren brushed away a sudden trickle of tears.

Two grubby little boys stood spellbound and silent in the doorway.

And upstairs Sarah listened and wondered.

Why, Sarah wondered, had she never heard of her cousin, Miss Percy? Why had Miss Percy come to Dunleith? What story was the music telling?

Mr. Dahlgren, when he came home from his bank, provided no answers for Sarah's questions though he indicated that he, too, was interested in the length of Miss Percy's visit.

"She brought just one little trunk," Sarah told Mr. Dahlgren, "so she must not plan to visit long. It's an old trunk, battered and scratched, that looks as if it has been on a long journey."

"No doubt it has," Mr. Dahlgren remarked. He said nothing else, leaving Sarah to wonder if he knew where the trunk—and Miss Percy—had been.

Sarah questioned the servants, but she learned nothing from them, nor were her friends able to provide her with information about Miss Percy.

It was Miss Percy herself who, several weeks later, satisfied Sarah's curiosity—or some of it.

Sarah walked into the parlor one afternoon when

Miss Percy was playing the harp. On this occasion, she was singing softly. Sarah listened and exclaimed,

"You're singing a French song!"

The music stopped, and Miss Percy looked inquiringly at Sarah. "Yes. I learned the song in Paris. Do you know it?" she asked.

Sarah did know the song (she had learned it during the months she studied in Europe), so together she and Miss Percy sang the French words.

As the song ended, Miss Percy placed her hand gently on Sarah's shoulder and said, "Thank you, my dear, for singing with me. It has been a long time since anyone has shared my music. I used to sing that song with someone I loved very much. He and I —"

Sarah leaned forward eagerly, impatient to hear what Miss Percy was about to say, but the greying lady stopped short, sighed and said only, "But that was a long, long time ago."

Then Miss Percy rose and hurried upstairs to her room.

Sarah sat alone in the parlor, going over in her mind the things Miss Percy had said and puzzling over the things Miss Percy had not said. She was trying to imagine Miss Percy young and in love when Mrs. Dahlgren came into the room.

"Mother, who was Miss Percy in love with?" Sarah asked.

"Miss Percy? In love? I—I really do not know his name."

Actually Mrs. Dahlgren was telling the truth: she did not recall the name of Miss Percy's lover. She— Mrs. Dahlgren—and others in Natchez who knew the story always referred to the man in Miss Percy's life as "that Frenchman."

Some older residents of the town said the man was a French count or duke. Others contended that he was a high-ranking officer in the French Army. Whatever his title or rank, he had accompanied Prince Louis Philippe (later to serve as King of France from 1830 to 1848) on a visit to Natchez in the early 1800s.

During the stay of the royal entourage in Natchez, Miss Percy met and fell in love with "that Frenchman." Their love affair was the talk of Natchez, and even Prince Louis Philippe is said to have taken an interest in their romance, referring to them as "that charmingly happy couple."

The two, Miss Percy and "that Frenchman," were not married during the foreigners' stay in Natchez nor was there an official announcement of their engagement, but he is supposed to have promised to send for Miss Percy as soon as conditions in unsettled France made it possible for her to join him there.

So Miss Percy waited. Months passed with no word from "that Frenchman." Then, when everyone except Miss Percy had concluded that the love affair was a mere flirtation and that the French visitor had never intended to send for Miss Percy, the letter arrived. Miss Percy shared its contents with no one, but its message made her ecstatically happy.

A week later she had packed a small trunk and had gone to New Orleans where she boarded a ship bound for France. Everyone in Natchez assumed, of course, that Miss Percy has gone to marry "that Frenchman," and they were delighted with this happy ending to a storybook romance.

Truthfully, not everybody was happy about Miss Percy's trip to France. Certain members of her family considered the journey entirely improper. No properly-reared young lady, they contended, went traipsing off without a chaperone to join a man who was not yet her husband. People close to the family said some of the Percys even told Miss Percy that the Frenchman would never marry her. There were, reportedly, heated words exchanged and ultimatums issued by older male members of the family.

Although this family unpleasantness may have cast a slight gloom over Miss Percy's departure, it did not for one minute lesson her determination to cross the ocean and join the man she loved.

Because they knew Paris is a long way from Natchez and they were aware that communications between the two points were chancy, Miss Percy's friends were not disturbed when they did not hear from her. At first they thought she was too excited and too busy preparing for her wedding to write. Later they decided perhaps she had been changed by her life as a member of the French court and that she no longer cared for her former friends.

"She's forgotten all about us," they said.

And after awhile, they forgot about her. Or most of them did.

Unfortunately, Miss Percy's life in France was

neither glamorous nor exciting. Nothing turned out the way she had thought it would. Her lover, so attentive and considerate in Natchez, became increasingly indifferent and surly in his native France.

At first he had seemed overjoyed to have her with him again. They explored the countryside together; they attended balls at court; they entertained small groups of his friends with their music, he singing to the accompaniment of her harp; they visited art museums and attended concerts; and they purchased clothes for her in shops more elegant than Miss Percy had ever imagined.

But they did not marry.

Always, it seemed, he found excuses for postponing the wedding plans. After awhile, he even refused to discuss marriage, and finally he told her, "I no longer find you amusing or entertaining. I wish you had never come to France!" Just how long it was before this final rejection came or how long she tried to reclaim his affections, no one in Natchez ever knew, but it was some years after her departure that Miss Percy quietly returned to Natchez.

Embarrassed to face her family, to hear their, "I-told-you-sos," Miss Percy turned to Mrs. Dahlgren, to whom she was connected by marriage, for comfort and for shelter.

In the Dahlgrens' imposing new home, Dunleith, showplace of Natchez, Miss Percy found refuge from prying eyes and gossiping tongues. There, too, she found solace in music.

She never left the house, but each afternoon she went downstairs to play the harp. The swish of her full skirts as she descended the stairs announced the daily concert, and often members of the family or servants would slip into the parlor to listen to her plaintive music. Playing the harp was her sole interest, for only in her music could she recapture the happiness she had once known or pour out the burden of a broken heart.

For Miss Percy's heart was broken. She still loved "that Frenchman," still longed to be with him.

If it is true that people can die of broken hearts, that is what happened to Miss Percy. One afternoon she failed to come swishing down the stairs to play the harp. When Mrs. Dahlgren went to see what had detained her, she found Miss Percy sitting motionless in a low rocking chair by the window. The doctor, who was quickly summoned, said she had been dead for several hours.

A few days after Miss Percy's funeral, Sarah walked into the hall and heard, coming from the parlor, the familiar strains of the duet she and Miss Percy had sung. She rushed into the parlor to see who was playing the harp, but as she entered the room, the music stopped.

No one was there.

"Mother!" Sarah called "I was sure I heard Miss Percy playing, but . . ."

"Yes, dear," her mother replied, "I heard her harp music, too."

That was the first of the ghostly late afternoon concerts Miss Percy gave on the haunted harp. For more than a century those concerts have continued. Residents of Dunleith still hear the swishing of long skirts followed by plaintive melodies from a harp as Miss Percy releases in music her love and her longing for "that Frenchman."

Miss Percy came to Dunleith for a long, long visit.

9

The Lovely Afternoon

VICKSBURG, MISSISSIPPI

*J*udge William Lake had taken his short afternoon nap, a custom of long standing with the Vicksburg jurist. He slipped on his coat, straightened his vest, and, after a few moments of searching, called, "My dear, do you know where my glasses are?" Mrs. Lake came into the bedroom where her husband had been resting. She walked unerringly to the tall dresser, picked up the glasses, and handed them to the judge.

"Thank you," he said. "I could not remember where I had laid them."

Mrs. Lake wondered, as she had wondered every

afternoon for a quarter of a century, how a man who could recall every legal detail of a complicated civil case could never remember where he had put his glasses. The glasses were always in the same place, always on the dresser, but always the judge summoned help to find them. The search for the glasses was as much a part of his daily routine as was his habit of rising from the dinner table and, after complimenting the quality of the heavy midday meal, announcing as though he were about to take some new and startling course of action,

"I believe I'll take a little nap before I go back to the office."

"Do, dear," she always replied. "I'm sure you need a little rest." She always used the same words.

During the half hour or so between the time the judge announced his intention of taking a nap and the time he called for assistance in finding his glasses, the house at the corner of Main and Adams was abnormally quiet: no doors slammed, all conversation was in whispers, all walking was on tiptoe. Only the clock in the upstairs sitting room continued its normal routine, and it was the sonorous striking of this timepiece that roused Judge Lake from his sleep.

This day Judge Lake, ready to return to his book-lined office, paused to bid his wife good-bye, just as he always did. "Good-bye, my dear. Have a lovely afternoon."

They were the words he always said, but this afternoon they sounded a bit different, a bit hoarse or husky. Mrs. Lake noticed the difference, slight though it was, and asked quickly, "Are you all right? Is anything wrong?"

He cleared his throat. "No. No–nothing is wrong. Good-bye, my dear. Have a lovely afternoon."

He kissed her lightly and walked out into the October afternoon.

It was, to all appearances, a farewell like thousands of others on thousands of other afternoons, but Judge William Lake knew it was different: this afternoon he was not returning to his office. He was going to fight a duel.

He wanted to look back, wanted to see again the way his house looked with the autumn sun shining on its galleries and balconies and gardens, but he was afraid his wife might be watching and might wonder at the gesture. She had caught a hint of something unusual in his farewell, and he did not wish to arouse her anxiety. He was pleased that he had been able to hide his own apprehension from her by following without deviation his normal routine.

He did not want Mrs. Lake to worry, did not want to spoil her afternoon. He remembered, walking down the steep hill toward his office, how she always delighted in her afternoons. Usually, after he returned to work, she rested and read a bit before dressing for the afternoon. Sometimes she went calling, riding in her carriage over the bumpy streets, to the homes of friends, and sometimes she entertained at her own home where she served her guests tiny beaten biscuits with quince jelly and dainty sandwiches or french pastries. He teased her about her fancy tea parties and laughed in amusement at the tid-bits of gossip ("crumbs from the party," he called them) which she passed along to him.

Every afternoon, weather permitting, she walked in her garden. She cut fresh flowers for the house, and she gave instructions to the gardner about planting, pruning, and cultivating the flowers and shrubs. Already, though several weeks of lingering summer warmth remained, they were making plans to move the tender plants—begonias, elephant ears, sultanas, and ferns—to the deep flower pit for the winter.

Mrs. Lake reveled in the beauty of her garden. "It restoreth my soul," she used to say, and in times of trouble she sought solace there.

Lately, Judge Lake recalled, she had less time for her garden. She had been busy with war work: embroidering battle flags, knitting, writing letters, preparing hospital kits and such. It was a war year, 1861, and the South, the Confederate States of America, was engaged in bitter combat with Union forces.

Mrs. Lake's conscience bothered her when she spent time in her garden instead of devoting her full energies to supporting "our gallant men in grey," but Judge Lake encouraged her to continue her strolls in the garden. He understood her need for the renewal which the garden provided.

Wherever she went during her afternoons, Mrs. Lake always left a lingering, gentle fragrance of haunting sweetness. For years, since Judge Lake brought her the first tiny bottle, she had used the same kind of perfume, a delicate and elusive blend of floral scents. Perhaps jasmine predominated. It was difficult to tell.

Judge Lake, that October afternoon, half fancied that the fragrance of his wife's perfume followed him along the sidewalk. It was a foolish fancy, of course. How much of the perfume did she have on her dressing table, he wondered. He tried to recall whether or not he had brought her a bottle when he returned from his last trip to New Orleans, but he could not. He hoped he had.

He passed the new courthouse, its columned porticos and tall cupola towering over Vicksburg, and he wondered if he would ever again appear in a courtroom there. "I must not think such morbid thoughts," he reprimanded himself.

But memories kept rushing in, demanding recognition. He passed the corner, where, as a young lawyer newly come to Vicksburg from Maryland, he had seen placards posted ordering the gamblers to leave town within twenty-four hours. That had been an exciting time. Even now he recalled vividly—had it really been a quarter of a century ago?—details of the episode and the feelings of tension that gripped the town.

He remembered the Fourth of July celebration which had been disrupted by the vulgar behavior of a gambler, a man named Cabler, who had come uninvited to the social affair. Cabler was ejected, but he returned later armed with a loaded pistol, a knife, and a dagger, and he vowed to kill the gentleman who had ousted him.

Cabler's vow of revenge was never carried out: he was taken into custody by a group of citizens, responsible men, who took him into the nearby woods where they lashed him, applied a covering of tar and feathers to his body, and ordered him out of town.

Encouraged by their success in ridding Vicksburg of one of its evil leeches, civic leaders called a public meeting to make plans for ousting all professional gamblers from their dens along the river. The law-abiding townspeople could no longer tolerate the gamblers' insolence, vulgarity, insults, thievery, and brutality.

The plan agreed upon was to inform the gamblers that they had twenty-four hours to get out of Vicksburg. Vigilantes would rout out any who defied the order.

Judge Lake had sharp recollections of that July morning in 1835 when a posse of citizens advanced on the house where five of the most notorious gambling sharks had barricaded themselves. In the brief skirmish there, Dr. Hugh Bodley, a young and beloved physician, was killed by a shot from the house. Enraged by the death of their friend, the Vicksburg vigilantes stormed the structure and took five men (Dutch Bill, Smith, McCall, North, and Hullums) into custody.

A short time later, five bodies dangled from five taut ropes.

Judge Lake recalled distinctly the tone of terrified disbelief in the voice of North when he cried out, "In the name of God, gentlemen, surely you are not going to hang us!"

The sigh of a tightened noose was his reply.

The judge remembered, too, how on the following day the five bodies were cut down and buried in a ditch.

"If death comes to me today," he thought, "at least I will be accorded a decent burial." Again he upbraided himself for harboring morbid thoughts.

Truthfully, Judge Lake did feel morbid. He dreaded the duel he faced. Unlike many of his friends, he found no glory or pride in defending honor on a private field of battle, and he secretly decried the punctilious code of conduct that demanded such action.

He had no desire to kill Mr. Chambers, his adversary. Mr. Chambers was his political opponent in a contest for a seat in the Confederate Congress, but, though the canvass was heatedly partisan, Judge Lake had no personal enmity toward the man. Certainly he did not want to kill him.

Yet somehow he had become involved in a situation that, according to the code of a gentleman's behavior, could only be settled by engaging in a duel. The challenge had been issued and accepted; the seconds had been named; the site and time and weapons (pistols at ten paces) had been agreed upon; and the surgeons had been notified to be present, all according to the precise and formal pattern required by the code duello.

How, Judge Lake wondered, had he allowed himself to be caught in the trap of senseless medieval chivalry? He was fifty-three years old, and he did not want to kill or be killed.

Yet already across the river on De Soto Point, seconds were making final arrangements for the duel. The sandy strip of land had been agreed upon as the site because of its strategic location. It was beyond the Mississippi boundary and therefore immune from interference by law officers from that state (dueling was illegal), and it was so far removed from any Louisiana town that arrest by Louisiana officers was highly unlikely. The Point had become a favorite dueling ground.

Plans called for the two adversaries, their seconds, and their surgeons to cross the river in separate boats and to meet at the Point for final instruction. Other boats were already crossing the stream as spectators gathered to watch the affray, and considerable money was being wagered on its outcome.

From the beginning, from the issuance of the challenge until that very day, Judge Lake's primary concern had been the fear that his wife would learn of the duel. She, gentle and sensitive, could never understand the necessity for mortal combat (how could he explain it to her when he himself could not justify it?), and the knowledge that her husband faced a duel would have caused her deep heartache, deeper than her garden could restore.

So Judge Lake had taken every precaution to keep the news of the duel from his wife. And on this afternoon, this lovely afternoon, as he walked toward the waiting boat, his only consolation was that she had been spared the sad knowledge of his involvement in a duel.

But she did know.

Mrs. Lake, after the judge had left the house, had rested a bit, and had then begun to dress for the afternoon. She had put on a silk dress (she loved the swishing rustle of the full skirt, and it rather amused her that she, a middle-aged married woman, should still find pleasure in such girlish trivialities), and she was touching her perfume to her throat, her temples, and her wrists when her maid burst into the room.

"Missus—It's bad news! The Judge is going to fight! He's on his way across the river. It's that man—Mr. Chambers—"

Mrs. Lake whirled around from the dressing table

and demanded, "What are you saying?"

As she started across the room toward the distraught woman, Mrs. Lake knocked over the bottle of perfume, and it spilled over on the dresser, ran down the sides and formed a tiny puddle on the pine floor.

"What are you saying?" Mrs. Lake demanded again.

The maid was too upset to reply immediately, but under Mrs. Lake's prodding she repeated her story. Word of the impending duel had come from the home of one of the seconds where a butler had heard it discussed by gentlemen enjoying their after-dinner drinks and cigars. The butler had told the cook who had passed the news along to the gardener who had whispered it to a maid down the street who had hurried to the Lake's servants' quarters with the tidings.

"I had to tell you, the maid sobbed. "How we go' stop him? Judge Lake ain't no fighter—he be killed sho'!"

"Hush!" Mrs. Lake snapped. "You're not to talk that way! Bring my opera glasses and come with me."

Perhaps, Mrs. Lake told herself as the two women climbed the stairs to the second floor of the house, the story was not true. Surely Judge Lake would have told her if he were going to fight a duel. But, deep in her heart, she knew he would have tried to spare her to worry and grief, that he would say, just as he had said, "Have a lovely afternoon, my dear."

Still the servants may have misunderstood, may have been mistaken.

Mrs. Lake, followed by her maid, went out onto the second floor verandah where they had a clear view of the river and of De Soto Point on the other side.

Even without the opera glasses, Mrs. Lake could see an unusually large number of boats crossing the river to the Point, and when she trained her glasses on the Point, she saw a crowd of men gathered there. She moved the glasses slowly from group to group, fearing to find a familiar figure.

Then she saw him. At the edge of the gathering, in close conversation with a man whom she also recognized, was her husband.

Mrs. Lake stood on the high porch and watched in silence as the second loaded a pistol and handed it to Judge Lake. She saw Judge Lake and Mister Chambers stand back to back, then step off the prescribed distance. She saw the white handkerchief drop, and she saw the twin puffs of smoke when the pistols were fired.

The smoke cleared. Judge Lake lay on the ground.

"Oh, God!" Mrs. Lake breathed. "Oh, God!"

"Come on, Missus. Let's go downstairs," the maid urged. "Don't look no mo'. Please don't look no mo'."

But Mrs. Lake could not move. She stood as though hypnotized with her glasses focused on the tragic scene across the river. She saw the surgeon kneel on the sand to examine Judge Lake, saw him rise and shake his head. She saw the seconds lift Judge Lake's body and place it in a boat.

As the craft started across the river, she dropped her glasses and walked slowly downstairs.

IT WAS MORE THAN a century ago that Mrs. Lake stood on the upstairs gallery that lovely afternoon and watched her husband's death.

The house is still there in Vicksburg at the corner of Main and Adams. The top story, where the ballroom and the guest bedrooms and the gallery with the view of the river were located, was destroyed by fire in 1916, but the lower floor retains its original design and charm.

The house has been restored by its present owner, John Wayne Jabour a young Vicksburg businessman, who purchased the property in 1973 from the heirs of B. Coccaro, a grocer, who acquired the place about 1900.

A few residents of the old Lake home have seen a shadowy figure strolling in the garden along the worn paths Mrs. Lake followed when she sought solace there, when she needed to restore her soul.

And each generation of occupants of the house has told of hearing, on lovely afternoons, the swish of silk skirts along the porch and in the garden and of smelling the tantalizing odor of exotic perfume, a haunting scent of flowers—jasmine, perhaps—such as Mrs. Lake used on lovely afternoons.

10

The Snake Charmer

Johnson County, Tennessee

Sometimes on summer nights, when moonlight softens the rough profiles of the Stone Mountains, snatches of fiddle music drift from Fiddler's Rock. The tunes change, blend, swell, fade, and swell again as though a distant fiddler were warming up for a performance.

Not everyone hears the music. And some mountaineers, especially the younger ones, say it is not music at all but the sound of wind rushing down from high rocks and swishing through the trees and losing itself in the twisting coves and hollows. Others say it is only the music from record players or radios bouncing against the cliffs and echoing into the valleys.

But other mountain dwellers hear the tunes plainly

and recognize the distinctive style of the fiddler.

"Listen," they say. "Listen. Old Martin is playing tonight. What's that? 'Cripple Creek'! Hear it? Just as plain. That's old Martin, all right. Up there charming his snakes. Bet that old rock is thick with rattlers now, crawling out of their dens to hear Martin play his fiddle. Old Martin. The snake charmer. Just listen . . ."

It has been better than a hundred years—closer maybe to a century and a quarter—since Martin lived up in Johnson County, Tennessee. Some folks say he was born near Trace, and others claim his family lived not far from Elk Mills.

Wherever it was that Martin was born, he grew up in those rugged east Tennessee mountains. He hunted and he fished and he trapped, when he wasn't helping his daddy cut logs. Long before most boys could even open a jack knife, Martin was whittling little wooden figures of animals—squirrels and rabbits and bears and such. His grandfather taught him how to see a creature in a piece of wood.

His grandfather taught Martin how to play the fiddle, too. He taught him to play the old tunes brought over from England, the staid hymns, the dancing play-party rhythms, and the wailing laments for times long past.

With his grandfather's help, Martin made his first fiddle, whittling it out of seasoned wood and carving decorations on it to suit his fancy.

By the time he was half grown, Martin had the name of being the best fiddler in Johnson County. He played for weddings, and he played for funerals. He played for barn raisings, and he played for church sociables. He played for dances, and he played for idlers sitting around the store down at the crossroads. He could play any tune anybody called for, and he made up a hundred or more tunes of his own.

"Tunes are just singing around in my head. I can hear them as plain as anything," Martin told folks who asked where he got his new melodies.

Neighbors used to say that if a restless, fretful baby was brought within earshot of Martin's fiddling, the baby would quit crying and drop off to sleep as peaceful as you please. It was like magic.

There was even some belief that Martin's music had curative powers, that it could make sick people well. Martin himself never made any such claims, though he was perfectly willing to go wherever he was asked to play for someone who was ailing.

"If my music helps them get well, that's fine. If it doesn't, at least maybe I've given them a little joyful time." Joyful times were important to Martin.

Up around Laurel Bloomery, they used to say that Martin had the only singing mule in the mountains. They said Martin would be playing his fiddle while he rode his mule, riding bareback the way he always did, and every now and then the mule would bray in time to the music. Some folks even said the mule's bray was in harmony with the fiddle and that anybody who was halfway listening could recognize the song the mule brayed. That could have been true. Maybe.

When Martin played for dances, they say listeners forgot their rheumatism and their stiff joints and were out on the floor stomping up a dust before Martin had played six measures of "Sourwood Mountain." "Even the preachers can't help dancing when Martin plays," they used to say.

People at Pandora, some of them, swore that Martin hunted with his fiddle. He used to go into the woods without a gun or any kind of weapon, just take his fiddle, and in a little while he'd come out with his hunting sack full of squirrels. All his pockets would be full, too. And not a one of those squirrels ever had a mark on them. Not everybody believed that tale.

But just about everybody who heard him play believed that Martin was the finest fiddler in east Tennessee. Maybe he was the finest fiddler in the whole state. Middle Tennessee wasn't much known for fiddling, and not many Johnson Countians had ever been as far as west Tennessee so they couldn't accurately judge. But in east Tennessee, where music was appreciated and respected, even the oldest fiddlers agreed that Martin handled the bow better than any musicmaker they'd ever heard.

Such praise didn't make Martin proud or strutified. "I can't paint pictures, and I ain't never made much success at farming, and I didn't do good in school, and I can't sing—not even as good as my mule can— and I can't make speeches. But the Good Lord talented me with fiddling. So that's how I want to be remembered: long after I'm dead and gone, I want folks to recollect how I played my fiddle."

Well, one afternoon Martin was sitting on the

edge of the store porch playing his fiddle, entertaining the idlers, when Absalom Stanley rode up and tied his mule to a post by the steps.

Soon as Martin finished playing the piece he had started, Absalom asked, "Martin, reckon you can charm snakes with your music?" Martin thought a minute, and then he said he never had once considered doing such a thing, and he didn't know if he wanted to try, and he wondered why Absalom would ask such a question.

"It's my boy, Polk. He wants to know," Absalom said. "He brought his geography book home from school, and that book tells about men somewhere— Indy, I think it is—who play little horns and charm snakes. Even make them dance. Soon as my boy, Polk, read that, he said, 'I bet Martin can charm snakes with his fiddle.' Can you?"

Martin didn't answer right away. Nobody had ever asked him such a question before. He sat there on the store porch studying about it. He laid his fiddle across his knees and picked the strings with his thumb and forefinger while he thought. He picked those strings a pretty good while, not making any kind of a tune, before he said, "Charming snakes ain't a easy thing to do. At least I don't figure it is. Never heard of anybody around here doing it. But maybe I can. Bring Polk's book tomorrow afternoon and let me read about it. Then I'll see what I think."

Then Martin took his fiddle and got on his mule and headed home.

News about Martin's upcoming decision spread fast, and the next afternoon there was a sizable crowd gathered on the store porch. Martin entertained them with music until Absalom got there with Polk's geography book.

Absalom handed the book to Martin, and Martin, though he wasn't the best reader in the county, read aloud the short paragraph about the Indian snake charmer.

The men were quiet as a cistern while Martin read, but as soon as he stopped, one of them asked, "You reckon that's really so? Reckon them men do charm snakes with their playing?"

"Must be so," Martin replied. "They got pictures here of a little old man squatting down on his haunches and playing a horn, and a funny looking snake is reared up right in from of him, looking him in the eye. It must be so."

He passed the book around for them all to see.

"Don't reckon that cloth wrapped around the fellow's head has anything to do with his power over the snakes, do you?" one of the men looking at the sketch asked. "Don't know as we could get Martin's head wrapped up like that!"

"It ain't the head-wrapping that bothers me," Martin replied. "I just wish I could hear a sample of the tune the man is playing. I don't know whether it takes a dancing tune or a doleful melody to charm a snake."

"You're gonna do it, then?" Absalom asked.

"I'm gonna try," Martin replied. "If snakes in Indy can be charmed, so can snakes in Tennessee. Snakes is snakes."

"When you aiming to do it?"

"Tomorrow, I reckon. Too late today, not enough daylight left. I'll set out in the morning, not too early, for that flat ledge up on the mountain. By the time I get there, the sun will be pretty high, and the snakes'll be coming out of their dens to stretch out on the rock ledge and warm themselves. I'll sort of ease in there, me and my fiddle, and see how they like my music."

One or two of the older men in the crowd cautioned Martin about fooling around with rattlesnakes, but Martin had made up his mind.

So the next morning Martin, astride his mule, set out with his fiddle to the Stone Mountains. He guided the mule up the steep path as far as the footing was safe. Then he tethered the animal to a stout sapling and continued to climb afoot.

Martin climbed over rough boulders and skirted deep crevices, brushing against clumps of rhododendron and laurel, until he reached the flat ledge where he intended to stage his experiment. Then he settled himself on a rock, a big one shaped like a footstool, near the center of the ledge and began to play.

He started off slowly, playing a gentle melody. Then he picked up the tempo, and he played a little louder, sort of coaxing the snakes out of their hiding places. Out of the corner of his eye, Martin saw a rattler ease out of a rock pile and glide toward him. Martin played a little louder and little faster. The snake—he was monstrously big—slid up closer and then stretched out full length on the gray rock.

Martin kept playing. He was careful not to pat his foot—and the naturalness of beating a rhythm with his foot was hard to control—fearing the movement might cause a snake to strike. Only his fingers on the strings and his hand wielding the bow moved. And his eyes: they moved almost constantly as Martin watched the arrival of other snakes who came to share the concert.

Pretty soon there were almost a dozen rattlers out on the ledge. They weren't exactly charmed, Martin decided, but his music had lured them out of their dens, and they were all still and quiet.

Martin knew, having grown up in the wilds, that snakes have no ears, so it stood to reason they couldn't hear the tunes he was playing. They were attracted, he decided, not by the beauty of his music but by the vibrations of the sound waves.

After awhile, Martin got tired: even the world's finest fiddler can't keep playing forever. He was uneasy, too, not knowing what the snakes would do if he quit playing. He gradually slowed the pace and the volume of his music until it trailed off into nothingness. Then he eased his fiddle and his bow across his knees and sat there as still as the stone he had chosen for his stage.

Maybe it was half an hour, maybe longer, before the snakes began to crawl away, heading back to wherever it was they had come from. Martin was muchly relieved: he didn't know what he would have done if they had decided to stay.

But they did leave, all except one. That one snake and Martin looked at each other for a long time. Finally Martin decided the snake was asleep (it's hard to be sure: a snake has no eyelids to close). Martin took a stout stick with a small fork on the end, and he quickly pinned the snake to the ledge. Then he crushed the writhing reptile's head with the heel of his boot.

He dropped the dead snake into his hunting bag, and he climbed down the mountain to where his mule was waiting.

As soon as he got in sight of the store, Martin could tell there was a big crowd waiting for him.

"Did you charm them snakes?" somebody hollered.

"Sure did!" Martin called back.

Martin sat on the porch and munched cheese and crackers (he hadn't realized how hungry he was) while he told his listeners everything that had happened.

Parts of his story he repeated half a dozen times. Then he showed them the snake he had brought back.

"He's not so big—most of them were a lot bigger," Martin said half apologetically.

The men measured the snake out on the floor, and the storekeeper measured it: five feet, eight and one-quarter inches, counting the rattles.

Martin took the snake home with him, skinned it, and tacked the skin up on the side of the smokehouse to dry. He dropped the brown rattles down into his fiddle as a sort of a good luck charm.

At first Martin thought one effort, and a rather successful one, to charm rattlesnakes would be enough, but it didn't satisfy the populace of Johnson County (seems that as word about the snake-charming spread, more and more people got interested in it), and it didn't fully satisfy Martin either.

So he went back again. Again he played for the snakes, and again they responded to his music. And again Martin brought back a big snake, quite dead, to show off at the store.

It finally got to where Martin was going up to the ledge three or four times a week to play for the snakes. He had a feeling sometimes that they were waiting for him, that they missed him when he didn't come.

A story got started around the region (whether Martin himself told it or not is uncertain) that the snakes—at least some of them—got to where they would shake their rattles in time to Martin's music.

Anyhow, Martin kept giving those concerts for a long time. His whole smokehouse was covered with the drying skins of trophies he brought home.

Then Martin got to wondering if the rattlers would come out to hear him play at night. He wondered about it for a week or two, and since there wasn't anybody to ask, he was determined to find out for himself.

One moonlit night, a warm night in early September, Martin followed the familiar trail up to the Stone Mountains to where the jutting ledge of rock formed a strange concert hall.

It was Martin's last trip up that mountain.

About daylight the next morning, a rider passing along the valley road heard a mule braying in a peculiar way. He found Martin's mule tethered on the slope of the mountain where Martin always left him.

A search party found Martin's body lying on the trail, about halfway down the mountain. Fang marks, more than two dozen of them, pocked his swollen hands and face. His fiddle was lying beside him, but the bow was missing.

While some of the men took Martin's body home, a few others continued the climb up the mountain to look around the ledge. These searchers found Martin's missing bow lying beside the round rock where Martin sat during his concerts.

Nobody is fully certain what happened. It appears that Martin got careless, just for an instant. He must have dropped his bow, reached down in the shadows to pick it up (he knew better—he momentarily forgot the potential deadliness of his audience), and been bitten by a rattler. Other reptiles joined in the attack, thrusting their fangs into the hands that had played for them, had tried to charm them.

They still talk about Martin up there in east Tennessee. His performances gave the name to the ledge high up on the Stone Mountains where he played to the snakes: Fiddler's Rock, natives call it.

And on summer nights when fiddle tunes drift softly from the isolated heights of Fiddler's Rock, folks who hear the music recall Martin and his music.

"Listen," they say. "Listen. It's Martin playing his fiddle to charm the snakes. I reckon he'll be playing up there forever."

11

The Witch Who Tormented the Bell Family

ROBERTSON COUNTY, TENNESSEE

*I*t all happened more than one hundred and fifty years ago, but the tales of the Bell Witch are still Tennessee's most famous ghost tales—and its most amazing.

John Bell, victim of the witch's hatred, was an unlikely subject for such a visitation. Born in North Carolina in 1750, he, his wife, and their children moved to Robertson County, Tennessee, in 1804.

Bell bought one thousand acres of land along the Red River, cleared fields, planted orchards, and built a sturdy house for his family. Nearby he built a one-room school where his children (Jesse, John, Drewry,

Benjamin, Zadoc, Richard Williams, Joel Egbert, Esther, and Betsy) and his neighbors' children were educated.

John Bell was a very religious man. Neighbors said his life was guided by the Bible and by the American Constitution with the most emphasis, of course, on the Bible. He had family prayers (kneeling) three times daily, and his house served as a gathering place for prayer meetings and other worship services.

On those occasions when he had business in town, he was an imposing figure in his long blue split-bottom coat trimmed with silver buttons, his beaver hat, and his linen stock. His fervent political speeches were credited with helping to win many elections, and he never hesitated to speak out for what he felt was right.

In short, John Bell became wealthy and influential with a reputation for genial hospitality, personal integrity, and Christian discipleship. There was certainly nothing in his background or in his personality to suggest that he would literally be tormented to death by a witch.

Bell first encountered the witch, as the spirit chose

to be called, in the late summer of 1817. He was walking through his corn field, estimating the possible size of his crop, when he saw a strange animal sitting between the rows. The creature, which looked like a dog, stared at Bell in a way that made the man feel uneasy. He shot at it and the animal disappeared among the thick corn stalks.

The episode would probably not have caused Bell any concern had not similar events followed.

Within the next few days one of Mr. Bell's sons, Drewry, saw a huge bird, much larger than a turkey, perched on a fence. A daughter Betsy, on an outing with the other children, reported seeing a little girl dressed in green swinging on the limb of an oak tree near the house. Dean, the trusted Negro servant, told of meeting a peculiar black dog at a certain spot in the road each night.

One summer night in 1818, little Williams Bell, who was only six or seven at the time, was awakened by having invisible hands grab his hair and jerk it with such force that he feared his head was being pulled off. His frightened screams were drowned out by shrieks from Betsy in her room across the hall. She, too, had felt her hair pulled by rough, unseen hands. It was the beginning of months of torment suffered by the lovely young girl who, with her father, became the major object of the witch's wrath.

John Bell, up to this point, had tried to ignore the supernatural happenings at his home. He did not wish to be ridiculed by his neighbors, he did not want to upset his own family by putting undue emphasis on the strange occurrences, he still hoped to find a logical explanation for the events—and each day he half expected the intruder to depart. However, when the unseen spirit terrified his children and seemed determined to do them physical harm, John Bell sought help from his close friend, James Johnson.

"I know you will find it difficult to believe," John Bell told his friend, "but a demon has taken residence in our house. I need your help in determining what is causing our trouble."

So James Johnson and his wife spent the night with the Bells. Johnson was a pious man, a lay preacher, and he led the family prayers and hymns before they all retired for the night.

No sooner had the household settled down than

the commotion began. That night the spirit demonstrated all her perverse tricks, like a naughty child showing off for visitors. There were knockings, scratching, gnawings, chairs turned over, chains rattling, covers snatched off, hair pulled, and faces slapped. Nor did the guests escape: the cover was pulled from their bed, and constant bumpings in their room made sleep impossible.

Mr. Johnson became convinced that the deeds were performed by a force which possessed intelligence, and he tried to talk with it. His initial efforts at communication were not successful, but a few months later his theory proved to be correct.

Greatly puzzled by the mystery, Mr. Johnson advised Mr. Bell to make his plight known and to ask other friends to come help with the investigation. From that time until Mr. Bell's death some two years later, the Bell family had a continuous stream of visitors, some neighbors and some from far away. Not one of them was able to rid the house of its hex or to explain the witch's powers.

The visitors, encouraged by Mr. Johnson, tried to entice the witch to talk, to tell what its mission was.

After a time it did begin to make a soft whistling sound when spoken to. Then the whistle changed into an indistinct whisper, and finally that whisper grew clear and strong enough to be heard and understood by anyone in the room.

News that the Bell witch could talk created even greater excitement and brought more visitors to the home. Among the visitors none was more famous or more interested in the phenomenon than was General Andrew Jackson, soon to be elected president of the United States.

Jackson was living at his home near Nashville at the time, and when he heard of the cavortings of the witch at the Bell home, he determined to go and investigate for himself. He rounded up some of his fun-loving friends to share the trip. They loaded camping equipment and provisions into a wagon (Jackson did not wish to impose on the Bells' hospitality as so many other visitors had done), and the men set out on horseback behind the wagon.

Jackson reined up his horse to call to a friend, "We're off on a witch hunt to John Bell's place. I'll bet you my best fighting cock against a keg of your best whiskey that the witch is a fraud!" And he rode off.

As the caravan neared the Bell home, the wagon suddenly became stuck on the dry, solid, ground. No matter how the driver urged the horses or how hard they strained, the wagon would not budge. Its wheels were locked.

Jackson and his friends dismounted and pushed with all their strength, but not an inch did the wagon move. The men removed the wheels to examine them closely, but they found no fault which could account for the stalled wagon.

"It must be the witch," Jackson said, half in jest.

From above the wagon came a caterwauling voice. "All right, General. Go on! I'll talk to you tonight." The wagon moved easily and quickly toward the Bell home.

Jackson paid his bet—he had found out that the witch was no fraud.

Meanwhile, the witch's conversations increased in frequency and in duration. She enjoyed amazing her listeners with her knowledge of the Bible and of religious matters. She could sing every hymn in the hymnal, could quote any passage in the bible, and could argue convincingly any question of theology.

She must have been a faithful if unseen attendant at church services, for she would often astound visiting preachers by repeating word for word their prayers, their hymns, their announcements, and their sermons. She was a talented mimic and could copy voices and inflections perfectly.

She particularly liked to mimic James Johnson whom she called "Old Sugar Mouth" because of the "sweet words he says when he prays and preaches."

Perhaps even more amazing than her interest in religion was her custom of reminding guests of events in their past, often happenings that had occured miles away. In fact, the witch began making nightly reports of all the doings in the community. Many residents, it is said, improved their conduct for fear their misdeeds would be reported publicly by the witch. She seemed to be able to be everywhere, see everything, hear everything and, most dangerous of all, tell everything!

Her religion was only on the surface, however, and did not prevent her from bedeviling Mr. Bell and Betsy unmercifully. She seems to have hated Mr. Bell and to have envied Betsy. The rest of the family she tolerated, and she even had real affections for Mrs. Lucy Bell.

Many examples are recorded of the witch's devotion to Mrs. Bell, but perhaps the most amazing show of concern came during a time when Mrs. Bell was ill with pleurisy. The witch (she was called Kate although nobody ever knew whether the spirit was male or female—the subject of its true identity was one topic the witch refused to discuss) visited Mrs. Bell each morning during her illness and tried to cheer her by singing to her.

One verse from a song sung daily by Kate ended with the words,

"Troubled like the restless sea,

"Feeble, faint and fearful,

"Plagued with every sore disease,

"How can I be cheerful?"

Neighbors nursing Mrs. Bell never failed to weep at the witch's plaintive, sweet rendition of the sentimental song.

It was during the same illness that Kate, the witch, brought Mrs. Bell a gift of hazelnuts to tempt her appetite. "Hold out your hands, Lucy, and I will give you a present," the witch's voice instructed.

A shower of hazelnuts fell from the ceiling into Mrs. Bell's outstretched hands. Then, when Mrs. Bell observed that she could not eat the nuts because they were not cracked, their shells were cracked by strong, unseen hands, and then placed carefully on the bed beside Mrs. Bell.

People in the room who witnessed the event looked in vain for openings in the walls or ceiling, but they found no crevice through which the nuts could have come.

A few days later they were equally amazed when a bunch of wild grapes, freshly picked from a swampy thinket, dropped gently on the bed beside Mrs. Bell.

"Eat your grapes, Lucy. They'll make you feel better," the witch instructed.

Mrs. Bell's recovery began almost at once.

But as Mrs. Bell improved, Mr. Bell's health became worse. He complained of a strange affliction. At first he had the sensation of having a stick lodged crossways in his mouth. This was not too upsetting since it occured infrequently and was of short duration, but as the witch's hatred for him increased, this ailment grew in seriousness.

Mr. Bell's tongue swelled until it filled his whole mouth, making it impossible for him to eat or speak for hours or even days at a time.

In addition, the witch tantalized him in other ways, sometimes snatching off his heavy work boots, no matter how tightly the laces were tied, and slapping him with such force that his face showed the distinct marks of a handprint and ached for hours.

And all the while Kate boasted that she intended to put John Bell in his grave.

Finally Mr. Bell's afflictions, coupled with the constant taunting threats of the witch, sent him to his bed, where he died on December 20, 1820.

His death, witnesses said, was caused by a potent poison which the witch boasted she had poured between his lips during the night. The poison was never identified (even the doctor called to attend the dying man could not classify it), but when a few drops of liquid from the cloudy vial were placed on the tongue of a cat, the creature whirled around, sprang crazily into the air, keeled over, and died.

And the witch's taunting laughter filled the room.

After the death of John Bell, Kate concentrated her devilment on young Betsy Bell.

Betsy, in her late teens, was an unusually pretty girl, taller than average and with a graceful carriage. Her eyes were blue and sparkling, and her flaxen hair was long and quite wavy. She was a bright, intelligent girl, always praised by Professor William Powell for her fine school work, and she had a happy, sunny disposition. Or she had until the witch began tormenting her.

Betsy and Joshua Gardner, a handsome young man whom she had known since childhood, were deeply in love. Their plans for marriage displeased old Kate, and she alternately pleaded with Betsy not to marry Josh ("Please, Betsy Bell, don't marry Josh") and threatened her with dreadful consequences if she became his wife ("If you marry Josh Gardner, you will both regret it to the end of your days").

And so on Easter Sunday, 1821, Betsy returned to a heart-broken Josh Gardner the engagement ring she had accepted from him only the day before.

He left the community before the week was out,

and the lovers never met again.

After a proper interval, Betsy married her former school teacher, William Powell and they apparently had a good marriage until his death seventeen years later. In 1875 Betsy moved to Panola County, Mississippi, to live with her daughter, and she died there in 1890 at the age of eighty-six.

With the death of John Bell and the termination of the romance between Betsy and Josh, the witch's evil reign in the Bell household ended.

But descendants of John Bell's family still talk about the strange visitation of the witch and of the turbulent distress she caused.

They call it "Our Family Trouble."

12

The Farmer Who Vanished

RURAL MIDDLE TENNESSEE

*I*n the late 1880s there appeared in the *Cincinnati Inquirer* a news story of the disappearance—vanishing would be more accurately descriptive—of David Lang from his home near Gallatin, Tennessee. The story created a sensation at the time, and nowhere was it read with more interest than at Gallatin. Folks there declared it never happened.

But the reputation of the *Inquirer* is so fine, the story it printed was so plausible, so complete with details and so convincing that even today many people believe that David Lang did live in Gallatin and that he disappeared. According to the story in the Inquirer and other accounts published through the years, this is what happened:

One warm afternoon in late September (September 23 is the generally accepted date), 1880, Mrs. David Lang was sitting on her front porch watching her two children play in the yard. Sarah, who was about ten, was making a playhouse around the roots of a big oak tree. She had carpeted her "rooms" with clumps of green moss, and she was constructing furniture from acorn cups, twigs, and bark. Her younger brother, George, was building pens to hold the wooden cows and pigs his father had carved for him. The children's play amused her briefly, but Mrs. Lang was impatient for her husband to finish his farm chores and take her to town.

"We'll never get there before the stores close," she complained to nobody in particular. She needed to buy material for a Sunday dress for Sarah (the child was wearing her old Sunday dress to school) and a shirt for George. And they both needed shoes.

Mrs. Lang rose from her chair and walked to the

edge of the porch. She was about to call Mr. Lang, although she knew it would make him angry, when he appeared around the corner of the house.

"I'm coming," he informed Mrs. Lang. "I just want to walk down to see about the horses. It won't take long." He took his watch out of the bib of his overalls and looked at it. "We'll get to town in plenty of time," he assured his impatient wife. Lang opened the gate and started across the pasture. The pasture stretched in a gentle slope away from the house. It was clean, open grassland without trees or bushes.

The farmer had gone only a short distance when a buggy turned in at the road leading up to his house. In the buggy were two businessmen from Gallatin, long-time friends of the family, who had come out to discuss a proposed land sale with Lang. One of the visitors saw Lang starting across the pasture, and he stood up in the buggy to call to him.

"David! Wait!" he shouted.

Mrs. Lang and the children watched as David Lang turned to wave and acknowledge the greeting of his friend.

Then David Lang disappeared. One minute he was

standing in his own familiar pasture waving at a friend; the next minute he had disappeared, vanished completely—and forever.

Mrs. Lang ran screaming from the porch out to the pasture. The children threw down their playthings and followed her. The two visitors jumped from their buggy, climbed the fence, and dashed to the spot where they had last seen Lang.

There was absolutely no sign of him.

The grass, short and dry in the early fall, was crushed down at the spot where David had turned to wave at his friends, and that patch of trampled grass was the only evidence that anyone had been in the pasture. As the startled, almost hysterical people watched, the grass slowly righted itself and stood stiff and tall. Now nothing remained to indicate that, moments before, a man had stood on the spot.

His family and friends began a frantic search for David Lang, but there was nowhere to look. There was no shrubbery or bushes, not even a clump of weeds, that could hide a man in the pasture. There were no wells or sinkholes or crevices in the earth.

Mrs. Lang dropped to her knees and began digging frantically into the earth where she had last seen her husband. The hard ground tore her fingers, and blood mingled with her tears to mark the fateful spot. The visitors finally led her gently back to the house where one of them sat with her and the dazed children while the other one went to fetch help from neighbors.

Neighbors came, many of them, but though they searched every foot of the Langs' farm and of the adjoining farms as well, they found no trace of the missing man. A well-digger brought his rig and began excavating at the spot where Lang disappeared, but he soon struck limestone and had to abandon the effort. Bloodhounds were brought out by the county sheriff. The dogs lost the trail in the open pasture, right where Lang had disappeared. When they reached that spot, they tucked their tails and whined so pitifully that the sheriff ordered them put into the wagon and taken back to town.

Although the search continued for days, not one clue as to Lang's whereabouts was ever found.

At night, every night for two weeks, Mrs. Lang and neighbors at her house (friends arranged to stay with the poor woman twenty-four hours a day—she was in no condition to be left alone) heard David Lang call for help.

"Help me! Please somebody, help me!" they heard Lang begging.

The cries seemed to come from the place where Lang disappeared, but though his family and friends, who did earnestly want to help him, listened hard and looked harder, they never found the source of the cries. Each night the voice became weaker and faint until it ceased to be heard entirely.

After several nights passed without Lang's voice being heard, Mrs. Lang agreed to have funeral services for her departed (she hesitated to use the word deceased, not being certain that he was) husband. It did not seem proper, somehow, to have a man's funeral while his voice was still audible.

The next spring, when the grass in the pasture came up fresh and green, nature marked the spot of David Lang's mysterious disappearance with a perfect circle of stunted brown grass some fifteen feet in diameter.

Years afterwards, Ambrose Bierce, the American

journalist-author who later disappeared as completely and almost as mysteriously as did David Lang, wrote about the Tennessean who vanished. He believed the story.

And, though reputable citizens of Gallatin have denied its truth for years, so do a lot of other people.

13

Long Dog

SURGOINSVILLE, TENNESSEE

*G*ot to grease that squeaking wheel tomorrow," the wagon driver said to his wife. "Don't think I can stand to hear it complaining another two miles! Should have stopped and greased it this afternoon, but there wasn't time; dark has already caught us as it is, and I don't know how far we have to go before we find a settlement or a campsite."

His wife, sitting on the hard wagon seat beside him, tried to ease his anxiety (she was a wise wife who understood him well and knew that, though he spoke of a noisy wagon wheel, his real concern was to find shelter for the night) by saying, "The squeaking isn't bad. I don't mind it. Listen. It seems to be saying, 'New home. New home. New home.' It's nice."

She turned around and called to their son in the back of the wagon, "Don't you like it, Alex? You hear the wheel talking about our new home in Tennessee, don't you?"

Alex didn't answer. He leaned his head against a cowhide trunk and pretended to be asleep.

"The boy is asleep. Must be plumb worn out," Alex's mother whispered to her husband. "Maybe the squeaking wheel just lulled him off to sleep. He must like it, too."

Alex didn't like the noise, didn't like it at all. He pulled his knit cap down over his ears, and then he covered them with his hands, but still he heard the rhythmic squeak of the wheel repeating and repeating, "Long Dog. Long Dog. Long Dog." Alex was frightened.

He had been listening—how many hours ago? how many miles ago?—when a man had warned his father, "If you're on the road at night, be on the lookout for Long Dog. He never has hurt anybody as I know of, but he sure has scared a lot of folks traveling along near Surgoinsville after dark! He's a ghost dog, you know."

Alex's father had laughed, as though he knew the stranger were joking. The stranger didn't laugh though, Alex noticed, and something about the look in the man's eyes made Alex uneasy.

The boy wanted to know more about Long Dog, but he was too timid to ask questions. He hoped his father would ask the questions that tumbled around in his mind, but his father did not appear to be interested or concerned about the stranger's warning. He stopped only long enough to get water for the horses and information about the trail ahead, not long enough to inquire about a ghost dog.

So Alex sat in the back of the wagon and listened to the wheel grind out the fearsome warning, "Long Dog. Long Dog. Long Dog." The monotony of the sound was hypnotic and, though he fought sleep, Alex nodded.

He waked suddenly as the wagon jolted over a big rock. He heard his father cursing the rock and the darkness, and he heard his mother say reassuringly, "We can't be far from Surgoinsville."

Alex stretched and tried to find a more comfortable position in the wagon.

Then he saw Long Dog. Loping down the dark road behind the wagon came the biggest dog Alex had ever seen. The dog wasn't so tall—he was long, long, and lithe and glowing.

"Papa! Papa!" Alex shouted. "It's Long Dog!"

His parents turned around to comfort Alex about what was obviously a bad dream, and they too, saw the animal coming toward them. Long Dog, running with a swift grace, had almost caught up with the wagon. His sleek body shone in the dark like the brilliance of reflected moonlight.

"Get away from here!" Alex's father shouted. "Get away, I say!"

The phantom dog paid no heed. He ran along by the wagon for a little piece, and then he reared up so he could look over the side. He didn't try to get into the wagon, just looked all around. He acted as if he were trying to see who was riding in the clattering vehicle. He didn't make a sound, not a sound.

The horses, sensing a strange presence, bolted and raced through the darkness. Alex's father strained back on the reins, locked the brake, and shouted to his frightened horses to halt their runaway pace.

"Whoa, now! Whoa!" he urged his team. "Hold on! Hold tight!" he called to his wife and son. For the moment, he was too busy trying to calm his horses and care fof his family to pay attention to Long Dog.

Alex braced himself against a heavy trunk in the wagon bed, and he squeezed his eyes tightly shut. Finally he felt the wagon slow almost to a stop, and he heard his father say, "It's all right now."

Quickly Alex climbed up to the front of the wagon and edged onto the seat between his parents. They all three looked behind them. Long Dog was squatting on his haunches back down the road a piece, just sitting there watching the wagon. The dog looked lonesome, Alex thought, and pitiful, too.

Alex began to cry, the first tears he had shed since they had left their home in the Carolinas. His mother pulled him to her, holding him close. His father reached over and tousled his hair and then let his strong hand remain on his head a moment, long enough to give Alex a feeling of reassurance and of blessing.

"Don't be scared," his mother said. Alex wasn't scared, not any more. He didn't know why he was crying except that his sadness was somehow mixed up with a strange ghost dog.

Later, when they finally reached Surgoinsville, his father told men there of their encounter with the luminous dog and of the runaway horses. Alex was afraid his father might tell about his tears and the men might think he was a sissy or a coward, but his father made no mention of the crying.

"That was Long Dog all right," one of the listeners said. "Lots of travelers have seen Long Dog along that stretch of road. I've seen him myself more than once." And he told the story of Long Dog, the story Alex had been wanting to hear.

As do many Tennessee tales, the story of Long Dog involves John Murrell, the notorious outlaw of the frontier.

It seems that back when Murrell was terrorizing the countryside with his bold robberies and his brutal murders, back in the late 1820s and early 1830s, a family was passing through East Tennessee on the way to a new home near Nashville.

They made camp for the night beneath a spreading white oak tree between Kingsport and Surgoinsville. While they were sleeping, Murrell and his gang (depraved men, all) fell upon the travelers and killed them. Murrell even strangled the faithful hound dog that tried to protect the family.

Some years later, possibly after Murrell had been imprisoned for his crimes, settlers traveling the old stage route to Nashville via Bristol, Rogersville, and Knoxville began to tell of seeing a mighty peculiar dog, a ghost dog, along the way.

The dog, they said, would come out of the thick shadows of a white oak tree near Surgoinsville, and he would run along beside their wagons, run without making a sound. Every now and then the dog would leap up on a wagon and sniff around.

"The dog acts like he's hunting for somebody he thinks a heap of," they said.

"What does he look like? Well, he sure doesn't look like any natural dog. He's long, more than twice as long as any dog you've ever seen. I'd say he's as long as a plow line. And he shines in the dark. It's sort of like he had maybe a dozen lanterns inside him shining through his skin. Or maybe it's like he's made out of a big hunk of foxfire. It's scary looking, all right."

All of the travelers who encountered the ghost dog told almost identical stories. Not everybody believed the stories. One of the doubters was young Marcus Hamblen, a husky eighteen-year-old who lived with his family near Surgoinsville.

"A ghost dog! If I ever saw such a glowing critter, I'd kill him and skin him and nail his hide up on the side of the barn. Or maybe I'd cut him up and use all the glowing light to go 'coon hunting on dark nights," Hamblen boasted. He didn't believe in ghosts of any kind.

Not long after he had made that boast, Marcus Hamblen (Hamblen County was named for his family) was walking home from a frolic one dark night. As he neared an old white oak tree, the ghost dog came trotting out of the shadows toward him.

Marcus snatched a rail from the fence beside the road. "Come on, old Long Dog! I'll kill you dead!" he warned.

Long Dog never slowed up, just came trotting right back toward Hamblen.

When the dog got close enough, Hamblen drew back with the fence rail and hit Long Dog as hard as he could.

The rail went clean through the luminous dog.

Hamblen forgot all his boasting. He dropped the rail and ran. Long Dog ran right along by him. Hamblen ran faster. So did Long Dog. Hamblen speeded up. So did Long Dog.

Hamblen ran until he didn't have a bit of breath left. He stumbled and sprawled out in the road. Long Dog squatted on his haunches right beside Hamblen and waited.

As soon as his breath and strength returned, Hamblen got up and ran again. Long Dog ran right along beside him. They ran down the road side by side, Long Dog adjusting his pace to Hamblen's, until Hamblen succumbed to exhaustion again.

Long Dog waited patiently beside the prostrate youth. When Hamblen caught his breath, off they went again.

This strange race kept up until Hamblen and Long Dog reached a particular spot in the road where, observers said, Long Dog always disappeared. That's what happened then: Long Dog completely vanished. One minute he was trotting along beside Hamblen; the next minute he was gone.

Hamblen stumbled home. He was considerably shaken by the experience.

That wasn't the last time Marcus Hamblen saw Long Dog, but it was the last time he ever tried to kill the ghost dog or to run away from him. In fact, as time passed, Hamblen grew fond of Long Dog and looked forward with pleasure to their infrequent encounters near the oak tree on the road to Surgoinsville.

Many people through the years saw that ghost dog, Long Dog, but probably nobody ever felt as friendly toward him as Marcus Hamblen did, and nobody ever told stories about him better than Hamblen did.

Hamblen used to end his stories by saying, "Long Dog didn't mean any harm. He never tried to hurt anybody though he did scare a lot of folks. That old ghost dog was just out there trying to find his murdered master. He must have loved his master an awful lot. I hope he found him—somewhere."

It has been a good many years since anybody up in

that part of Tennesse has seen Long Dog. Maybe the road has changed or maybe people drive by too fast now.

Or maybe Long Dog has been reunited with his master, the way Marcus Hamblen hoped he would be.